DECEMBER 1997

Sunday	Monday	Tuesday	Wednesday	Thursday	Friday	Saturday
	1	2	3	4	5	6
7	8	9	10	11	12	13
14	15	16	17	18	19	20
21	22	23	24 Christmas Eve	25 Christmas Day	26	27
28	29	30	31 New Year's Eve			

In the years to come, you'll be glad you noted the special times of the season on these pages.

Christmas
with Southern Living
1997

Oxmoor House

Christmas
with Southern Living
1997

Edited by Rebecca Brennan,
Julie Fisher, and Adrienne E. Short

©1997 by Oxmoor House, Inc.
Book Division of Southern Progress Corporation
P.O. Box 2463, Birmingham, Alabama 35201

Southern Living® is a federally registered trademark belonging to
Southern Living, Inc.

Library of Congress Catalog Card Number: 96-68891
ISBN: 0-8487-1556-X
ISSN: 0747-7791
Manufactured in the United States of America
First Printing 1997

Editor-in-Chief: Nancy Fitzpatrick Wyatt
Senior Homes Editor: Mary Kay Culpepper
Senior Foods Editor: Susan Carlisle Payne
Senior Editor, Editorial Services: Olivia Kindig Wells
Art Director: James Boone

Christmas with Southern Living 1997

Editor: Rebecca Brennan
Recipe Developer: Julie Fisher
Assistant Editor: Adrienne E. Short
Associate Art Director: Cynthia R. Cooper
Editorial Assistant: Cecile Y. Nierodzinski
Copy Editors: Keri Bradford Anderson, Anne Dickson
Senior Photographers: Jim Bathie, John O'Hagan
Senior Photo Stylists: Kay E. Clarke, Katie Stoddard
Photo Stylist: Linda Baltzell Wright
Director, Test Kitchens: Kathleen Royal Phillips
Assistant Director, Test Kitchens: Gayle Hays Sadler
Test Kitchens Home Economists: Susan Hall Bellows,
Julie Christopher, Michele Brown Fuller, Natalie E. King,
Elizabeth Tyler Luckett, Jan Jacks Moon, Iris Crawley
O'Brien, Jan A. Smith
Illustrator: Kelly Davis
Publishing Systems Administrator: Rick Tucker
Production and Distribution Director: Phillip Lee
Associate Production Manager: Theresa L. Beste

Front cover: Chocolate-Orange Cream Cake, page 88
Back cover, top left: Winter Blooms in Painted Pots, page 114;
    top right: A Glittery Garland, page 20; bottom: Garland Wreath,
    page 12

We're Here for You!
We at Oxmoor House are dedicated to
serving you with reliable information that
expands your imagination and enriches
your life. We welcome your comments and
suggestions. Please write us at:
  Oxmoor House, Inc.
  Editor, *Christmas with Southern Living*
  2100 Lakeshore Drive
  Birmingham, AL 35209

To order additional copies of this
publication or any others, call
1-205-877-6560.

CONTENTS

Foreword

This season, actress and author Dixie Carter hosts "Our Holiday Memories," a one-hour television special from *Southern Living*. Here, she shares Christmas memories from her Tennessee childhood.

Dixie Carter and her father Halbert Carter

Christmas. FOR MANY OF US THIS WORD CALLS UP CHERISHED MEMORIES, happy anticipation of the next time this festive season rolls around, and bittersweet longings for the way it can never seem to us again. I experience the anticipation, the memories, and the longing each year. Christmas always had to do with the getting ready for, as much as the day itself, and that had to do with my mother, Virginia Hillsman Carter. Her preparations for the great day began way in advance and had a ritualistic quality to them, as do most of the occasions that mean a great deal to us.

Nothing was thrown together in a hurry. The fruitcake ingredients she began steeping a month in advance. The country ham was soaked for days to take the salt out, then simmered for two days on top of the stove in a big long copper pot that covered two "eyes." The ham was cooked at so low a temperature that you could put your hand in the water without getting a burn. The other cakes were started Christmas week. There was the puncturing of the coconuts with a hammer and nail, then the draining of the coconut milk, with mock annoyance at anyone's attempt to get a sip of it. (It had to be saved to go into the cake and icing!) There was the grating of the coconuts, which no one much wanted to do, since a skinned knuckle was a hazard for the careless grater. There was orange grating for the orange cake. There was nut picking for the nut cake. There was the mysterious double boiler, then spinning and drip-testing to arrive at the perfect chocolate fudge, then cooling and carefully cutting on wax paper. There would be also Aunt Fostina's white divinity fudge as a bonus.

Yet to come were the perfectly baked, not-dried-out turkey, giblet gravy, and our mother Gina's divine "dressing," which everybody calls stuffing now. She made it with fresh, hot cornbread and biscuit, and that *was* last-minute! Everyone in the house would be asked to render a verdict on whether or not it had enough sage in it. Plus cranberry sauce, cranberry jelly, asparagus casserole, sweet potato casserole, pickle relish ("mixed pickle"), spiced peaches and apricots, beautifully delicate butter beans, baked apples, and tiny light-as-air biscuits. When Uncle Tom and Aunt Naomi came, they brought her tomato aspic.

By the time Christmas Eve came, all was in readiness for the arrival of the magic Christmas ingredient: my mother's baby sister, Helen. Aunt Helen would swirl in from the cold, loaded with gorgeously wrapped boxes she would let us shake before she put them under the tree. She looked beautiful, smelled beautiful, wore wonderful-feeling garments, and adored her nephew and two nieces. Sometimes our Uncle Jack, my mother's older brother, would make the trip from Knoxville, and always there were both our grandmothers. But it was almost always my mother who read "The Night Before Christmas" to us, before we were wrapped in warm blankets and tucked into bed.

The gifts were usually under the tree for a long time—those from me and my brother and sister. We planned them way in advance, wrapped them, and put them under the tree so we could look at them, shake them, and try to guess what they might be. Often they were something that had caught our eye on the back of a cereal box.

The tree was one we had all gone out into the woods and cut down, with the permission of the landowner. The decoration of the tree was a grand ritual, everyone participating, unknotting and testing the many strings of lights from the attic, my mother exhorting us to hang the icicles individually. Clumps of icicles were beneath contempt. We loved it when my brother would sling a handful at the top of the tree, and Gina would wail in horror.

The house was decorated with holly and holly wreaths. On Christmas Day, Daddy would give each of us children a box of chocolate-covered cherries, which we were allowed to eat as we chose, all at once if we wanted. Santa Claus was strong on books; we loved the reading-and-candy-eating days after Christmas almost as much as the day itself.

Santa Claus always came. Even the two Christmases when Daddy was in Europe in World War II, and simply everything was rationed or impossible to get, Santa Claus managed to make it to our dear house in McLemoresville, Tennessee.

The last time I was home, I happened to see two of Santa's wartime gifts in the storage shed behind the barn. There they were, handmade toy chests, painted brown, with brass latches, and our names painted on the front. I still remember how thrilled I was that Christmas morning to see my little chest—how magical it seemed. Surely it had come straight from Santa's workshop! I was absolutely right. The nights my mother must have stayed up late after we went to bed, carefully sawing, nailing, gluing, sanding, determined to produce something special for her children, war or no war. Santa's workshop in truth.

I love Christmas as a deeply religious occasion, and as our most treasured family holiday. I will always feel my mother's hand on every Christmastime.

Christmas always had to do with the getting ready for, as much as the day itself . . .

ALL THROUGH THE
HOUSE

Evergreen Christmas

Joe Gordy knows how to decorate for the holidays. His real talent, though, is making Christmas last forever.

With a client list that includes Ronald and Nancy Reagan, Louise Mandrell, Eddie Murphy, Nick Nolte, and Sidney Sheldon, Joe Gordy is arguably the country's master of permanent—they're far too gorgeous to be called "artificial"—flowers and plants. Joe and his wife Carol's company, Natural Decorations, Inc., makes amazingly realistic fabric foliage arrangements that are featured at stores such as Dallas's Neiman Marcus and Gump's in San Francisco and are sold to high-profile customers around the world. The success—and beauty—of Joe's creations is directly attributable to their being absolutely botanically correct. As Joe says, "You'll never see a blue rose in our catalog."

He practices what he preaches when it comes to his stucco-and-brick Tudor-style home in Brewton, Alabama. At Christmas-time, Joe hangs a wreath on the door, fills vases and urns with greenery, and trims the tree with hundreds of family ornaments. As he deftly puts a twist here or a sprig there, he makes

seasonal decorating—with either permanent or real greenery—look easy.

It *is*, he insists, and he demonstrates just how easy over the next few pages. Watch as Joe shows step-by-step how to create a stunning topiary that features both fresh and permanent plants, and reveals the many uses of a garland that he embellishes using glue—and a lot of imagination. Then see how he utilizes what he finds in his own backyard to crown his work with natural glory.

The dining table garland (previous page) is a simple evergreen garland that Joe trimmed with permanent fruits, fresh camellia blooms, and gold cording. It surrounds a glorious display of fresh flowers and foliage. At dinnertime, the large arrangement can be set aside, leaving the adorned garland to serve as a centerpiece.

The lamppost garland is exquisitely adorned with similar permanent flowers and ribbons. (For Joe's step-by-step instructions, see page 11.)

Lamppost Garland

A Simple Garland

You will need:

purchased evergreen garland (Joe used a tapered garland that is fuller in the center; however, a straight garland will work as well.)
hot-glue gun and glue sticks
variety of ornaments, fruits, and foliage
wire-edged ribbon
florist's wire

1. To begin, reshape evergreen garland, straightening branches and fluffing them apart.

2. To add embellishments, hot-glue your choice of ornaments, fruits, berries, etc. to garland, gluing largest pieces at center of garland and using smaller pieces toward ends. (Be sure to cut hangers from ornaments.)

3 & 4. To make ribbon loops, fold an 8" to 10" length of ribbon in half, pinch-pleating cut ends together. Wrap ribbon ends with florist's wire to secure. Hot-glue ribbon loops to garland. For the wreath, use wire-edged ribbon to tie a bow. Glue or wire in place. (For bow-making instructions, see page 153.)

Garland Centerpiece

The **garland centerpiece, garland wreath,** and **lamppost garland** are all made from one simple embellishment idea.

For the wreath, Joe attached the garland to a wire wreath form to hang on his front door. (To shape the form to fit his door, he gave the unadorned round frame a big bear hug—it became a perfect oval.)

Joe used two garlands to
wrap the lamppost.

Variations on a Theme

Joe bases many of his holiday decorations on permanent evergreen garlands.

To begin, Joe suggests selecting a color theme to help unify your decorations. To dress up his garlands, Joe selected an assortment of permanent sugared fruits as the theme of his designs. To the fruits, he added gilded pods, pinecones, berries, and ribbons. For the larger garlands, such as the ones used for the wreath and the lamppost, his additions are more abundant. The garland centerpiece and the banister garland are more simply adorned.

In addition to the garland's many uses, an added bonus is the ability to use it year after year. Each Christmas, you can add more embellishments to it, creating a holiday decoration that grows more beautiful every time you use it.

Even the tabletop topiary follows the garland theme as fresh vines twine around a mossy cone (see page 15). And like all of Joe's work, it can be used again. To save it for next Christmas, Joe simply removes any fresh pieces from the cone, leaving vines and permanent pieces in place. When he brings it out again, he fills in spaces with fresh plants and foliage.

For directions on making the topiary, see page 14.

Banister Garland

On the banister, Carol intertwined the evergreen garland with a eucalyptus garland, adding wired ribbon and gold cording for sparkle.

A Topiary with All the Trimmings

You will need:
Styrofoam cone
florist's pins
hot-glue gun and glue sticks
moss
monofilament (fishing) line
blocks of dry florist's foam or Styrofoam
container
dowels or long florist's picks
vine clippings (can be clipped outdoors or from a
    grapevine wreath)
variety of ornaments, fruits, berries, fresh and
    permanent flowers and plants

Note: For Styrofoam, see Sources on page 154.

1 & 2. To cover cone, use florist's pins or hot-glue gun to attach moss to cone, completely covering cone. Knot 1 end of a long length of monofilament line around florist's pin and stick pin into cone. Wrap moss-covered cone with monofilament line to neaten shaggy edges of moss. Continue wrapping line several times around cone, making sure to cover point at top of cone. Use a florist's pin and a dot of hot glue to secure ends of line to cone. Use scissors to trim moss at bottom of cone, if necessary.

3. To prepare container, place florist's foam or Styrofoam blocks in container, making sure foam is level at top of container.

4. To place cone on container, position cone on top of foam blocks in container. Cut ends of 3 or 4 dowels or long florist's picks diagonally. With dowels or picks, pierce through cone into foam blocks to secure cone to container.

5. To add vine clippings, clip ends of vine diagonally and, starting at bottom of cone and working toward top, insert ends into cone, forming a large loop. Insert remaining vine lengths into cone in the same way, creating loops on all sides of cone. Insert a few shorter lengths of vine at bottom of cone, pointing down, and a few at top, pointing up.

6. To add embellishments, beginning at base, stick longest pieces of foliage into cone; working up cone, insert increasingly shorter pieces toward top. Continue adding your choice of decorations to fill out topiary. Most pieces can be stuck into cone to secure. If desired, use florist's picks or hot glue to secure pieces.

Topiary

Nature Is the Best Designer

"One of the best resources for plant materials in the South is our own backyard," Joe says.

Joe admits that his design talents are a God-given gift, but he relies on a few good principles that can help those with more down-to-earth abilities. First of all, don't be afraid to mix fresh flowers and foliage with permanent ones. "For parties, it's easy to stick in a few fresh blooms to enhance the permanent arrangement," Joe says. Secondly, take advantage of native plants. "One of the best resources for plant materials in the South is our own backyard," Joe says. Berries, twigs, even shrubbery clippings, blend together beautifully and are especially appropriate for seasonal designs. Once you gather your backyard treasures, Joe advises, "Let nature tell you what to do."

Fraser fir is Joe's choice for the longest-lasting fresh tree. His ornaments are a miscellaneous collection gathered on trips and given to him by friends.

Red peppers are the element of fun Joe likes to use inside and outside the house. **Pepper lights** swirled on a yaupon holly topiary get the patio in the holiday mood.

The mantel arrangements in Joe and Carol's home are fine examples of his design philosophy: they include yaupon holly, leucothoe, mountain laurel foliage, succulents, spider plant, lavender cotton, and clippings from the family Christmas tree. Joe used moistened florist's foam tucked into matching urns to contain his clippings and help keep them fresh.

Four amaryllis bulbs in a container on the coffee table contribute to the festive feel in the living room. Joe said it "just happened" that each of the bulbs bloomed at exactly the same time. We can only wonder.

For our tips on growing amaryllis, see page 114.

Braid Cuff Stocking

Shimmering Satin Stockings

Cuffed with velvet cording or golden braid, these sumptuous stockings are for those who have been especially nice.

You will need (for 1 stocking):
pattern and diagrams on page 145
graph paper with 1" grid
⅝ yard satin
⅝ yard 45"-wide fusible interfacing
1 package tear-away stabilizer
3 yards metallic cording (for braid cuff)
3½ yards velvet cording (for velvet cuff)
12 decorative beads (optional)
metallic thread (optional)

Note: All seam allowances are ½", unless otherwise noted. For velvet cording and beads, see Sources on page 154.

1. **To make stocking,** using graph paper, enlarge and transfer stocking pattern to stocking fabric. From satin, cut 2 stocking pieces. Reverse pattern and cut 2 more. (You will use 2 stocking pieces to make lining.) From interfacing, cut 2 stocking pieces.

Following manufacturer's directions, fuse interfacing to wrong side of 2 stocking pieces. With right sides facing and raw edges aligned, stitch stocking pieces together, leaving top edge open. Clip curves, turn, and press.

To make lining, cut 2 (8½" x 2") interfacing pieces, and fuse 1 interfacing piece to top (wrong side) of each lining piece. With right sides facing and raw edges aligned, stitch stocking lining pieces together, leaving top edge open and 4" opening in side seam for turning. Clip curves. Do not turn. Press.

2. To make cuff, on tear-away stabilizer, draw a 16" x 2" rectangle. Draw horizontal line across center of rectangle (1" from top and 1" from bottom), forming seam allowance line. Mark ½" seam allowance at each end of rectangle. Make additional marks on rectangle as follows: make first mark 2" from end of rectangle; from this mark, measure and make marks in 3" intervals across rectangle. (***Note:*** For velvet cording, make marks at 2½" intervals.)

Cut 5 (18") lengths of metallic cording. (***Note:*** For velvet cording, cut 6 (17") lengths.) Fold each length of cording in half; center ends of each folded piece on each mark on stabilizer, aligning ends with top of stabilizer (see Diagram 1). With ends of cording even with top of stabilizer, stitch cording to stabilizer close to 1" seam line (approximately ⅞" from top).

To create cuff design, hand-sew centers of each cording section together at center of each loop. Stitch centers of newly formed loops to centers of neighboring loops, as shown in Diagram 2.

When all available loops are formed, sew short ends of stabilizer together at ½" seam allowance lines to form a tube. Hand-sew remaining loops.

Turn cuff so that stabilizer is on top. (Cuff will be right side out.) Pin cuff to right side of stocking at top. Baste cuff to stocking at 1" seam line. Remove tear-away stabilizer.

3. To form hanger, cut 10" length of cording and fold in half. With raw edges aligned, baste ends of cording to right side of stocking at side seam.

4. To sew lining to stocking, with right sides facing, slip lining over stocking and cuff unit, matching side seams and top edges. Stitch lining to stocking around top edge at 1" seam line, catching ends of hanger in seam. Turn stocking through opening in lining. Stitch opening closed. Tuck lining inside stocking. Turn cuff down.

5. To add beads, run a single metallic thread through bead and tie around hand-stitches, allowing bead to dangle in center of loop opening. At top tier, sew bead thread loop to stocking.

**Velvet Cuff
Stocking**

A Glittery Garland

Surround your tree or wrap your mantel with a frothy twist of tulle and ribbon. It's wonderful something this versatile can be made in minutes.

You will need (for 6' garland):
2⅓ yards 6"-wide bronze tulle
2⅓ yards 6"-wide gold-flecked ivory tulle
2⅓ yards 1½"-wide white iridescent wire-edged ribbon
2⅓ yards 6"-wide gold tulle
2⅝ yards ¼"-diameter wired metallic cording

Note: We used 5 (6') garlands to decorate the tree pictured. For tulle, see Sources on page 154.

1. **To make garland,** on a large, flat surface, layer bronze tulle, gold-flecked ivory tulle, ribbon, and gold tulle, beginning with bronze tulle and ending with gold tulle. Starting at one end of tulle, measure in 3" from end and mark with a pin. From that mark, measure 18" and mark with another pin. Continue measuring and pinning 18" increments down the length of layered tulle and ribbon.

2. **To secure tulle,** with cording, tie a knot around all layers of tulle and ribbon at first 3" pin mark. Remove pin. Wrap cording around garland approximately 3 times to hide knot. Loosely wind cording around garland once, wrapping cording tightly around garland 3 times at second 18" pin mark. Remove pin. Continue loosely winding cording around garland and tightly wrapping 3 times at each pin mark until you reach end of garland. Remove pins. Secure end by knotting cording as at beginning of garland. A 3" length of tulle will remain past knotted end of cording.

Wrapped-in-Gold Ornaments

Tulle and cording color these shining ornaments, which coordinate beautifully with the garland, opposite.

You will need (for each):
3" Styrofoam ball
wire-edged ribbon
florist's wire

For Tulle-Wrapped Ornament:
gold spray paint
4 yards 6"-wide tulle

For Cord-Wrapped Ornament:
6 yards cording
low-temperature hot-glue gun with glue sticks

Note: For Styrofoam balls and tulle, see Sources on page 154.

For each Tulle-Wrapped Ornament: Spray a Styrofoam ball with gold paint. Let dry. Cut 8 (17") strips of tulle. Stack the strips into 4 double-layered tulle strips. On a flat surface, stack 2 double-layered strips to form a cross. With the remaining 2 double-layered strips, form a cross and place it diagonally atop the first cross.

To cover with tulle, place the ball in the center of the strips and wrap the tulle around the ball, gathering the ends at the top of the ball. Secure the tulle ends with a rubberband. To finish, tie a ribbon around the tulle ends, covering the rubberband.

For each Cord-Wrapped Ornament: Pin 1 end of cording to the bottom of the ball. If needed, secure the end with a drop of hot glue. Beginning at the bottom of the ball and working to the top, wrap the cording around the ball, hot-gluing cording to ball as you wrap. Let dry. Pin the end of the cording at the top of the ball. To finish, tie the ribbon into a bow; hot-glue the bow to the top of the ball.

For each ornament hanger: Form a 2" length of wire into a U-shape. Insert wire in the top of the ball.

Glamorous Velvet Throw

Transform plain velvet into a figured fantasy with an iron and a rubber stamp. Use it to make a table runner, pillows, or a mantel scarf. Or, follow these directions to create this luxurious throw.

Imprinting Velvet

You will need:
rayon velvet (in desired yardage)
water in mister bottle
rubber stamp with bold design (Detailed stamps do not print well.)
ironing board
iron

Note: For rubber stamps, see Sources on page 154.

To imprint velvet, generously mist the right side of the velvet. Place the stamp (rubber side up) on an ironing board. Lay the fabric, right side down, on top of the rubber stamp. Set the iron on wool setting. Do not use steam. When the iron has warmed to the proper temperature, press the velvet on top of the stamp. Hold the iron firmly in place and count to 20. (If the image is not as distinct as you would like, press for an additional 10 seconds.) Continue pressing the pattern on the fabric in this manner to achieve the desired design. The velvet may be dry cleaned, when necessary.

Velvet Throw

Note: Finished throw is 44" x 53", excluding fringe. All seam allowances are ½".

You will need:
1½ yards imprinted velvet
1½ yards lining (We used satin.)
5⅝ yards fringe

1. To cut out throw, cut 1 (45" x 54") velvet piece and 1 (45" x 54") lining piece. With scissors, starting 2" before corners and ending 2" after corners, round corners of velvet and lining. If desired, zigzag or serge all raw edges to make handling easier.

2. To add trim, lengthen stitch length and loosen presser foot tension (if possible) on your sewing machine; this will make stitches smoother. With right sides facing, align top edge of fringe with raw edge of velvet and stitch in place around all edges. Trim excess fringe so that beginning and ending edges abut after stitching.

3. To sew throw, with right sides facing and raw edges aligned, on velvet side, stitch along previous stitching line on all edges, leaving 8" opening for turning. Turn throw and stitch opening closed. Press lightly on satin side, if necessary.

Mary O'Neil from Nashville, Tennessee, is enthusiastic about the stamping technique she developed. Mary says, "This is the most exciting and rewarding craft I have ever delved into. I am totally addicted to the satisfaction I get from every impression I make to achieve this rich and luscious fabric."

Ribbon Wreath

Make this traditional wreath to suit any room in your house by choosing just the right combination of ribbons and embellishments.

To make the wreath, choose a Styrofoam wreath of the desired size. Wrap the wreath form tightly with 1"- to 2"-wide ribbon, overlapping ribbon slightly. (*Note:* Ribbon yardage will vary according to the diameter of the wreath. Wrapping the wreath form with a tape measure will aid in calculating the amount of ribbon needed.) Secure the ribbon at the back of the wreath with glue or with straight pins.

There are a variety of ways to embellish the wreath. Fruit picks, pinecones, silk greenery, and ribbons are a few examples. For our wreath, we hot-glued ribbon roses to the wreath and tucked in a few pinecones and berries for color and texture. The large bow is made from wire-edged ribbon, which you can attach to the wreath with wire or hot glue. On the back of the wreath, use straight pins to secure a length of ribbon to use as a hanger.

Note: For directions to make ribbon roses and the large center bow, see page 153. For the Styrofoam wreath and ribbon, see Sources on page 154.

Old-Fashioned Christmas Soaps

Soaps decorated with holiday stickers bring a festive
touch to the guest bath.

You will need (for each):
**aluminum foil or wax paper (to protect work
   surface)**
large tin coffee can (for double boiler)
household paraffin
smooth bar soap
stickers
tongs

Note: For stickers, see Sources on page 154.

1. **To protect work area,** cover surface with
aluminum foil or wax paper.

2. **For double boiler,** place empty coffee can in
large pot of water on stove burner. Melt paraffin in
can over low-medium heat. Carefully watch and
keep paraffin over heat as you work.

3. **Before decorating soap,** smooth surface of
soap under warm water, if needed. Dry soap.
Position sticker on soap, smoothing any wrinkles in
sticker with fingertips.

4. **To cover soap with paraffin,** carefully dip
sticker side of soap into melted paraffin, holding
soap with tongs. Carefully remove soap to protected work surface.
Let paraffin dry. If desired, apply another layer
of paraffin to this side of soap to fully coat; let
paraffin dry. Leave other side of soap uncoated so
it can be used.

Star Billing

The sky's the limit when you decorate ordinary household items with a celestial-inspired stamp. Copy the star pattern we show here, or make up your own.

You will need:
patterns on page 144
1 white craft foam sheet
scissors
craft glue
cardboard pieces
paintbrushes: medium and fine
acrylic paint
acrylic fabric painting medium (only if stamping on fabric)
objects to be stamped (We used chandelier shades, cotton napkins, sheets, and a glass canister.)

1. **To make stamp,** use ballpoint pen to transfer pattern to craft foam. Using scissors, cut out pattern pieces. Referring to pattern for placement, glue foam pieces to cardboard pieces that have been cut just larger than the pattern. Let dry. On back of stamp, mark top center with an arrow to ensure accurate positioning when stamping.

2. **To apply paint,** use medium paintbrush to apply paint to stamp. Referring to manufacturer's directions, add fabric painting medium to acrylic paint to stamp on fabric. Thoroughly cover stamp design with paint.

3. **To stamp,** press stamp firmly against surface and hold in place for a few seconds, being careful not to let stamp slide. (**Note:** If necessary, use fine paintbrush to fill in spots in design.) Reapply paint to stamp after each application.

Note: **For chandelier shades,** press stamp on 1 edge of design and roll stamp to other side.

For napkins and bed linens, before stamping, wash and dry fabrics. (Do not use fabric softener.) Press. Place a large cardboard piece under fabric. Stamp desired pattern. Let dry completely, and then press to set paint.

Napkin

Bed Linens

Glass Canister

Chandelier
Shades

A HOLIDAY BRUNCH

Many great flavors and make-ahead opportunities abound in this midmorning menu. And you can choose between casserole or quiche, bread pudding or pastries.

Grapefruit Compote in Rosemary Syrup

Cinnamon-Raisin Bread Pudding

Country Ham Scones with Maple Butter

Menu
Serves 10

Grapefruit Compote in Rosemary Syrup

Southern Brunch Casserole *or*
Three-Cheese Spinach Quiche

Orange-Cream Cheese Pastries *or*
Cinnamon-Raisin Bread Pudding

Country Ham Scones with Maple Butter

Ambrosia Punch   Coffee

Southern Brunch Casserole

Ambrosia Punch

Grapefruit Compote in
Rosemary Syrup

*Prepare and refrigerate Southern Brunch Casserole, the filling for Orange-Cream Cheese Pastries, and Maple Butter the day before your brunch.
*Slice oranges for the punch bowl, and section grapefruit for the compote. Seal the fruits in zip-top plastic bags, and store them in the refrigerator overnight.

Grapefruit Compote in Rosemary Syrup

Citrus and rosemary make quite an impression when they mingle in this honey syrup. You'll want to savor the syrup as much as you'll want to eat the plump fruit. Serve this refreshing first course in goblets or footed dessert dishes.

1   cup sugar
½ cup water
3   tablespoons honey
3   sprigs fresh rosemary
6   large grapefruit
½ cup maraschino cherries with stems
    Garnish: additional fresh rosemary sprigs

Combine first 4 ingredients in a saucepan. Bring to a boil over medium heat. Boil 5 minutes. Remove from heat, and let cool completely. Remove and discard rosemary.

  Peel and section grapefruit over a serving bowl to catch juice. Add grapefruit to bowl. Pour rosemary syrup over fruit in bowl. Add cherries. Cover and chill until ready to serve. Garnish, if desired. **Yield:** 10 servings.

The whimsical fruit garland (at right and on previous page) is really not hard to make. Just string lady apples, kumquats, and Key limes on florist's wire. Find lady apples at a gourmet grocery store or farmers market in the fall, or see Sources on page 154. Find Key limes prepackaged in net bags with other citrus fruit at the grocery store.

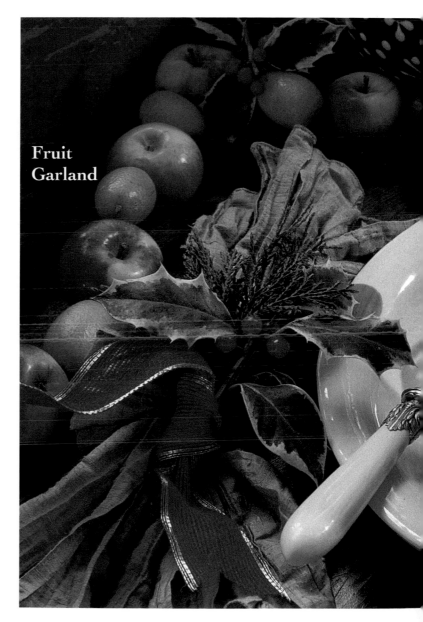

Fruit Garland

Southern Brunch Casserole

cheese, Italian seasoning, and pepper, stirring constantly until cheese melts. Remove from heat.

Layer half each of egg slices, bacon, and cheese sauce in a lightly greased 13" x 9" x 2" baking dish. Top with potatoes. Top with remaining egg slices, bacon, and cheese sauce.

Combine breadcrumbs and 3 tablespoons melted butter; sprinkle over casserole. Cover and chill overnight, if desired.

Remove casserole from refrigerator. Let stand at room temperature 30 minutes. Bake, uncovered, at 350° for 30 minutes or until thoroughly heated. Garnish, if desired. **Yield:** 10 servings.

Note: A mushroom slicer makes a neat and easy job of slicing hard-cooked eggs for this recipe.

Three-Cheese Spinach Quiche
Red and green rise to the top of this creamy quiche that has a flaky crust.

- ½ (17¼-ounce) package frozen puff pastry sheets, thawed
- 1 (10-ounce) package frozen chopped spinach
- 1 cup whipping cream
- ¼ teaspoon salt
- ½ teaspoon pepper
- 3 large eggs, lightly beaten
- 1½ cups (6 ounces) shredded mozzarella cheese
- ½ cup (2 ounces) shredded Cheddar cheese
- ½ cup finely chopped onion
- 1 (7-ounce) jar roasted red peppers, drained and chopped
- ½ cup (2 ounces) crumbled feta cheese

Unfold pastry sheet onto a lightly floured surface. Roll into a 13" square. Place in a lightly greased 9" deep-dish pieplate. Fold edges under, and crimp. Prick pastry lightly with a fork. Freeze at least 15 minutes to make pastry firmer. Bake pastry at 400° for 12 minutes. Let cool on a wire rack.

Reduce oven temperature to 350°. Cook spinach according to package directions. Squeeze spinach between several layers of paper towels to remove excess moisture. Combine spinach, cream, salt, ½ teaspoon pepper, and eggs, stirring well.

Sprinkle mozzarella and Cheddar cheeses and onion into pastry shell. Add spinach mixture. Top

Southern Brunch Casserole
Make no mistake. This is a hardy dish—bubbling full of bacon, eggs, and sharp Cheddar.

- 2 large baking potatoes, unpeeled and cubed
- ¼ cup butter or margarine
- ¼ cup all-purpose flour
- 1 cup milk
- 1 cup half-and-half
- 4 cups (16 ounces) shredded sharp Cheddar cheese
- 1 teaspoon dried Italian seasoning
- ½ teaspoon pepper
- 12 hard-cooked eggs, sliced
- 1 pound bacon, cooked and coarsely crumbled
- 2 cups soft whole wheat breadcrumbs (4 slices bread)
- 3 tablespoons butter or margarine, melted
  Garnish: fresh herbs

Cook potatoes in boiling water to cover in a large saucepan 15 minutes or until just tender. Drain and let cool.

Melt ¼ cup butter in a heavy saucepan over medium-low heat; add flour, stirring until smooth. Cook, stirring constantly, 1 minute. Gradually add milk and half-and-half; cook over medium heat, stirring constantly, until thickened and bubbly. Add

Grapefruit Compote in Rosemary Syrup

Orange-Cream Cheese Pastries

Three-Cheese Spinach Quiche

with red pepper; sprinkle with feta cheese. Bake, uncovered, at 350° for 55 minutes or until set. Cover loosely with aluminum foil, and let stand 30 minutes before serving. **Yield:** one 9" quiche.

Note: You can use ½ (15-ounce) package refrigerated piecrusts instead of puff pastry in this quiche, but it won't be as flaky.

Orange-Cream Cheese Pastries

These gooey caramel biscuits deliver a sweet cream cheese-coconut filling. They're rich, but you'll still eat more than one.

```
1   orange
1   cup firmly packed brown sugar
¾ cup whipping cream
½ cup butter or margarine
1   cup chopped pecans
1   (8-ounce) package cream cheese, softened
3   tablespoons powdered sugar
2   tablespoons butter or margarine, softened
½ cup flaked coconut
2   (12-ounce) cans refrigerated flaky biscuits*
```

Grate 1 tablespoon rind from orange; set rind aside. Squeeze ¼ cup juice from orange. Combine juice, brown sugar, whipping cream, and ½ cup butter in a saucepan. Bring to a boil over medium heat. Boil 3 minutes. Remove from heat, and let cool slightly. Pour mixture into a greased 13" x 9" x 2" baking dish; sprinkle with pecans. Set aside.

Combine reserved orange rind, cream cheese, powdered sugar, and 2 tablespoons butter in a small mixing bowl. Beat at medium speed of an electric mixer just until blended. Stir in coconut.

Separate biscuit dough into 20 pieces. Quickly roll each biscuit on a lightly floured surface to a 4" circle. Spread 1 tablespoon cream cheese mixture onto center of each biscuit circle. Roll up, jellyroll fashion. Place biscuits over brown sugar mixture in dish, seam side down, in 2 long rows.

Bake, uncovered, at 350° on lowest rack in oven for 32 minutes or until browned. Let cool in dish 5 minutes. Carefully turn pastries out onto a large serving platter. Top with any remaining brown sugar glaze. **Yield:** 20 pastries.

*We used Hungry Jack biscuits in this recipe.

Cinnamon-Raisin
Bread Pudding

Cinnamon-Raisin Bread Pudding

*Use the whole loaf, even the crusts and end pieces, in
this spiced bread pudding plumped with extra raisins and
sweetened with maple syrup.*

> 4 large eggs, lightly beaten
> 1½ cups milk
> ⅔ cup maple syrup
> ½ cup whipping cream
> ⅓ cup firmly packed brown sugar
> 1 tablespoon vanilla extract
> 1 teaspoon ground cinnamon
> ½ cup raisins
> 1½ (1-pound) loaves day-old cinnamon-raisin
>   bread
>   Powdered sugar
>   Garnish: cinnamon sticks
>   Additional maple syrup

Combine first 7 ingredients in a large bowl; stir in
raisins. Cut bread into 1" chunks; add to egg mixture in bowl. Stir gently. Cover and chill overnight.

Pour soaked bread mixture into a lightly greased
9" springform pan. Place springform pan on a jellyroll pan.

Bake, uncovered, at 350° for 50 to 55 minutes
or until a knife inserted in center comes out clean.
Let cool in pan 10 minutes. Carefully remove sides
of springform pan; sprinkle bread pudding with
powdered sugar. Garnish, if desired. Cut into
wedges, and serve warm with additional maple
syrup. **Yield:** 8 to 10 servings.

Note: You can bake this in a 9" square pan or an
11" x 7" x 1½" baking dish if you don't have a
springform pan. Servings will be squares instead of
wedges.

Country Ham Scones with Maple Butter

Maple Butter
- ½ cup butter, softened
- 2 tablespoons maple syrup
- 2 tablespoons finely chopped pecans, toasted

Beat butter and syrup in a small bowl at medium speed of an electric mixer until fluffy and blended. Stir in pecans. Cover and chill. **Yield:** ⅔ cup.

Note: Don't be tempted to add more flour to the scone recipe. Scone dough should be a bit sticky.

Ambrosia Punch

Oranges can have varying shades of flesh. Pick two varieties (such as navels and red navels or blood oranges) to perch on the rim of your punch bowl for a contrasting garnish (see photo, page 29).

- 2½ quarts orange juice
- 2 cups pineapple juice
- 1 cup cream of coconut
- 2 small oranges, thinly sliced and halved
- 3 cups vanilla ice cream
- 3 cups ginger ale
- ½ cup flaked coconut, toasted (optional)

Combine first 3 ingredients in a punch bowl. Cut a slit halfway through each orange slice, and perch slices around rim of punch bowl. Add tiny scoops of ice cream to punch bowl; add ginger ale. If desired, sprinkle some coconut over punch; serve remaining coconut in a small dish. **Yield:** 4 quarts.

Country Ham Scones with Maple Butter

Salty slivers of country ham are woven into these tender and flaky rustic biscuits. Smear a dab of Maple Butter on top, and watch it melt.

- 1¾ cups all-purpose flour
- 2 teaspoons baking powder
- ½ teaspoon salt
- ¼ cup yellow cornmeal
- 2 tablespoons sugar
- ¼ teaspoon pepper
- ¼ cup plus 2 tablespoons cold butter, cut up
- ¾ cup slivered cooked country ham
- 1 cup whipping cream
  Maple Butter

Combine first 6 ingredients in a bowl; cut in butter with a pastry blender until mixture is crumbly. Stir in ham. Add whipping cream, stirring with a fork just until dry ingredients are moistened.

Turn dough out onto a lightly floured surface; knead 3 or 4 times. Transfer dough to a lightly greased baking sheet. Pat into a 7" circle. Cut into 10 wedges. (Do not separate wedges.)

Bake at 425° for 24 to 26 minutes or until scones are golden. Let cool slightly. Separate wedges; serve warm with Maple Butter. **Yield:** 10 servings.

Ambrosia Punch

Ribbon-Trimmed Tablecloth

TABLE MATTERS

Set the mood for celebration
with a stylish table. Ribbon-trimmed
table linens, painted glassware,
and wire-adorned tabletoppers create
an impressive backdrop for the
year's finest soirees.

Wire-Wrapped
Candles

Ribbon-Trimmed Table Linens

Festive plaid ribbon trims these table linens in holiday colors. Adapt this design for other special occasions with different ribbons.

Ribbon-Trimmed Tablecloth

You will need:
diagrams on page 148
round tablecloth
18 yards 1½"-wide ribbon (for 60" round
    tablecloth)

Note: For ribbon, see Sources on page 154.

1. To mark placement for ribbons, fold tablecloth in half and in half again. Press folds to crease. Open tablecloth right side up. Between each creased quarter mark, fold up edge of tablecloth toward center. Press to crease lines, marking placement of first set of ribbons on tablecloth (see Diagram 1).

2. To sew first set of ribbons, from ribbon, cut 8 (56") lengths. Turn under cut end of 1 length and place at edge of tablecloth. Align long edge of ribbon with 1 creased line. Topstitch ribbon along 1 long edge, trimming excess at ribbon end, if necessary, and turning under end of ribbon. Topstitch along opposite long edge of ribbon. (*Note:* Topstitch each side of ribbon in same direction to keep ribbon from puckering.) Topstitch 1 ribbon length to tablecloth along remaining 3 creased lines. (You will use 4 of the 8 ribbon lengths in this step. See Diagram 2.) Press stitched ribbons.

Ribbon-Trimmed Tablecloth

3. To sew second set of ribbons, fold tablecloth in half and in half again to mark another set of quarters between corners of ribbon box (see Diagram 1). Press folds to crease. Open tablecloth right side up. Between each creased quarter mark, fold up edge of tablecloth toward center across ribbon box. Press to crease lines, marking placement for second set of ribbons. Topstitch remaining 4 (56") lengths to tablecloth as in Step 2. (See Diagram 2.)

4. To make bows, from remaining ribbon, cut 8 (24") lengths. Tie each length into a bow. Safety-pin 1 bow to each inside corner where ribbons meet on tablecloth (see photograph).

Ribbon-Trimmed Napkin

You will need (for each napkin):
dinner napkin
2½ yards 1½"-wide ribbon (for 20" square
    napkin)

To make a ribbon-trimmed napkin, place the inside edge of the ribbon onto the napkin ¾" from the napkin edge. Pin to hold. Topstitch along the ribbon edge onto napkin, mitering ribbon at corners. Turn under raw edge and stitch ribbon ends together; trim excess.

Button-Trimmed Napkin

You will need (for each napkin):
dinner napkin
1 (⅞"-diameter) button to cover
1½" square of ribbon

To make a button-trimmed napkin, following manufacturer's directions, cover the button with ribbon. Stitch the covered button to 1 corner of the napkin.

Napkin Ring

You will need (for each napkin ring):
1 (½") PVC-DWV coupling (found in plumbing
    section of hardware stores)
24" (1½"-wide) ribbon
24" (1½"-wide) ribbon for bow (optional)
hot-glue gun and glue sticks

To make a napkin ring, glue 1 end of ribbon inside the coupling. Wrap the ribbon around the coupling at a slight angle, completely covering the coupling. Glue the end of the ribbon inside the coupling. Leave the napkin ring plain or make a bow from remaining ribbon and glue it to the outside of the napkin ring, if desired.

Napkin Ring
with Bow

Ribbon-Trimmed Napkin

Napkin Ring

Button-Trimmed Napkin

Striped Glass Cake Dome

A few quick strokes of glass paint dress up a plain cake dome for the holidays. If you can paint your fingernails, you can master this simple design.

You will need:
diagram on page 144
1 pedestal cake plate with clear glass dome
black felt-tip pen
newspaper (to protect work surface)
1 jar water-based textured paint for glass
paintbrush
gold dimensional paint

Note: For paint, see Sources on page 154.

1. To plan design, trace outline of glass dome on scrap of paper. Divide circle into equal pie sections (the dome pictured has 16 sections; see diagram). Turn glass dome upside down. Using paper sketch as a guide, on inside of dome, mark a line for each section with felt-tip pen.

2. To paint design, turn dome right side up and place on protected work surface. Using black lines as a guide, trace sections with glass paint on outside of dome. Fill in alternate sections with glass paint. Let dry at least 24 hours. When dry, outline sections with gold paint. Let dry. If desired, paint freehand design on unpainted sections as shown. Let dry.

Note: Paint will look opaque when you first apply it, but it will dry to a translucent finish.

To wash ink from inside of dome, wipe glass with damp cloth.

Lelia Gray Neil of Chapel Hill, North Carolina, says her love of giving handmade gifts comes from her mother. Lelia learned very well under her mother's tutelage, as is evident in the fanciful cake stand and painted plates shown here. "Mom always made Christmas a creative family affair," she says. "Every year we made decorations that have become lasting memories of very special holidays."

Painted Holly Place Settings

This holly-and-berry motif brings a casual air to holiday dining. The plates are a cinch to paint. You don't even have to stay within the lines!

You will need:
pattern on page 144
clear glass plates
newspaper (to protect work surface)
tracing paper
masking tape
enamel glass paint: red, green, black
small paintbrush
white chargers

Note: The enamel glass paint we used is dishwasher-safe. For paint, see Sources on page 154.

1. **To begin,** wash and dry plates before painting. Cover work surface with newspaper.

2. **To make pattern,** trace holly-and-berry pattern onto tracing paper. For each plate, referring to photo, position pattern facedown where desired on top of plate. Secure pattern with small piece of tape. Turn plate over on work surface so that bottom of plate is faceup.

3. **To paint design,** outline pattern onto plate using paintbrush and black paint. Let dry. Turn plate over and remove pattern. Following Step 2 and referring to photo, reposition pattern on plate and outline pattern with paint. Repeat steps 2 and 3 until you have painted complete design onto plate.

4. **To paint holly and berries,** on bottom of plate, use paintbrush to paint over holly leaves with green paint and berries with red paint. Let dry.

5. **For each charger,** referring to photograph and using paintbrush and black paint, paint small ½"-long scallops around outside edge of charger. Let dry.

Wire-and-Bead Candle Holders

Wire Napkin Rings

Wire-Wrapped Tabletoppers

Here's a clever yet inexpensive way to jazz up plain accessories. You can't go wrong—just let your creativity uncurl.

Salt and Pepper Shakers

Embellished Serving Pieces

Cruets

Individual Salt and Pepper Shakers

Wire-Wrapped Candles

To get started, you will need your choice of **accessories,** assorted gauges of **solder wire** (found at hardware stores and home centers), **beads, clear silicone,** and **needle-nose pliers** to aid in bending the wire. You can find beads at craft stores and in the craft department of many discount stores. (For beads, see Sources on page 154.)

Using the photographs as a guide, bend and wrap wire around each serving piece, creating loops and swirls where desired. To add beads, thread the wire through the beads and continue wrapping. Use fine-gauge wire to dangle beads, or glue beads in desired positions. Where necessary, use silicone to secure wire to accessories. Let dry for 24 hours.

Stained Glass Holly Cake

Peppermint Pretzel Wreath

Mini Cinnamon Roll Wreath

Cinnamon-Nut-Caramel Apple Wreath

Assorted Appetizer Wreath

Gingerbread Ring

WREATHS TO RELISH

Recipes follow for seven rings of wonder, each with a distinctive personality and flavor. These delectable decorations won't hang on your front door, but they won't stay on the table long, either.

String-of-Lights Cookie Wreath

Mini Cinnamon Roll Wreath

Many minirolls make this gooey pull-apart breakfast wreath.

1 cup water
1 cup milk
2 (16-ounce) packages hot roll mix
¾ cup butter or margarine, softened
⅓ cup sugar
2 large eggs, lightly beaten
¾ cup butter or margarine, melted and divided
¾ cup ground red cinnamon candies
⅓ cup sugar
1½ teaspoons ground cinnamon
Vegetable cooking spray
3 cups sifted powdered sugar
⅓ cup milk
Additional red cinnamon candies

Combine water and 1 cup milk in a saucepan. Cook over medium heat until mixture reaches 120° to 130°.

Combine hot roll mixes, yeast packets, ¾ cup softened butter, ⅓ cup sugar, and eggs in a large bowl. Add hot milk mixture; stir well. Cover and let stand 5 minutes.

Divide dough into 4 portions. Place 1 portion on a floured surface (keep remaining portions covered in refrigerator). Roll 1 portion of dough to a 20" x 7" rectangle. Brush with 3 tablespoons melted butter. Combine ground cinnamon candies, ⅓ cup sugar, and ground cinnamon; stir well. Sprinkle one-fourth of candy mixture over dough. Roll up dough, jellyroll fashion, starting at long side. Pinch seam to seal. Cut into ½" slices.

Place a 6" round cakepan in center of a 15" pizza pan. Spray both pans with cooking spray. Begin arranging cinnamon roll slices around cakepan on pizza pan, piling up roll slices several layers deep. Repeat entire procedure 3 times with remaining dough, melted butter, and candy mixture. (Keep pans in refrigerator when working with remaining portions of dough.)

Let roll wreath rise in a warm place (85°), free from drafts, 30 minutes or until doubled in bulk. Bake at 350° for 30 minutes or until golden. Cool slightly. Remove cakepan from center of wreath.

MAKING THE WREATH

▲Grind red cinnamon candies in a mini chopper (left) or food processor; or place them in a zip-top plastic bag, seal bag, and crush with a rolling pin (right).

◄Arrange cinnamon roll slices around a 6" cakepan, piling them several layers deep. If you don't have a 6" cakepan, use anything ovenproof that's a 6" circle, like a large soup bowl.

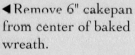

◄Remove 6" cakepan from center of baked wreath.

Combine powdered sugar and ⅓ cup milk; stir well. Drizzle over warm rolls. Sprinkle with additional candies.

Transfer wreath carefully to a large serving platter or cutting board, if desired. If rolls become separated, readjust them on the platter. Serve rolls warm. **Yield:** one 15" wreath (about 130 minirolls).

String-of-Lights Cookie Wreath

This thick, creamy vanilla frosting brightens our best-ever shortbread cookie. The dough works best using half butter and half margarine.

> 1 cup butter, softened
> 1 cup margarine, softened
> 1 cup sifted powdered sugar
> 4 cups all-purpose flour
> 1 teaspoon baking powder
> ½ teaspoon salt
>   Plastic drinking straw
>   Frosting
> 20 to 25 chocolate-flavored candy coating drops, melted
>   Small pastry brush or paintbrush
>   Red or black licorice, cut into 8" strips
>   Several 20" x 30" sheets of green tissue paper or Christmas fabric

Beat butter and margarine at low speed of an electric mixer until creamy; gradually add sugar, beating well. Combine flour, baking powder, and salt; add to butter mixture. Mix at low speed until blended. Roll dough to ⅜" thickness on a lightly floured surface.

Cut out cookies, using a 3" spade-shaped cookie cutter (or use template on page 149). Place on ungreased baking sheets. Make a hole in "socket end" of each cookie, using a straw.

Bake at 350° for 16 minutes. Let cookies cool on wire racks.

Spread Frosting on the "bulb end" of each cookie, using the back of a small spoon. Place frosted cookies on wire racks to dry. When frosting is dry, brush "socket end" of each cookie with melted chocolate, using a small brush. Let dry. When cookies are completely dry, lace licorice strips through holes in cookies. Place tissue in a large flat box, if desired. Arrange cookies in a loose circle on tissue paper to resemble a string of Christmas lights. **Yield:** about 2½ dozen.

Note: Use these cookies as tree ornaments or as edible place cards at a children's party. Write names on frosted cookies, using tubes of decorating gel.

Frosting

> 7 cups sifted powdered sugar
> 1 (5-ounce) can evaporated milk
> 1 teaspoon vanilla extract
> 25 vanilla-flavored candy coating drops, melted
>   Paste food coloring

Combine first 3 ingredients in a large microwave-safe bowl; stir well. Gradually add melted vanilla-flavored drops, stirring slowly to avoid air bubbles. Microwave at HIGH 45 seconds or until thin enough to spread; stir well. Divide frosting equally among four shallow bowls. Tint frosting to desired colors, using paste food coloring. **Yield:** 3 cups.

PREPARING THE COOKIES

◄ Make a hole in "socket end" of each cookie, using a drinking straw.

◄ Spread colored Frosting on "bulb end" of each cookie, using the back of a small spoon.

◄ Lace licorice through cookie holes, and arrange cookies in a loose wreath to resemble a string of lights.

MAKING THE WREATH

▲Place a single layer of coated pretzels around edge of serving tray.

▲Stack coated pretzels until the wreath is about 3" high.

▲Spoon small dots of melted candy coating onto top of wreath to act as "glue" for peppermints.

Peppermint Pretzel Wreath

Easy to make, hard to resist. This is one of those addictive salty-sweet snacks, and the addition of crushed peppermint makes it even better.

- 1 (24-ounce) package vanilla-flavored candy coating
- 1 (10-ounce) package large thin pretzels*
- 1 (6.75-ounce) package peppermint candies, crushed
- 7 additional peppermint candies
- 5 small Christmas bows (optional)

Place candy coating in a large glass bowl, and microwave at HIGH 1½ minutes or until coating melts, stirring once. Dip pretzels into candy coating, covering completely. Place coated pretzels on wax paper; sprinkle heavily with crushed peppermint. Let dry.

Place a single layer of pretzels around outside edge of a 12" serving tray. Continue layering remaining pretzels until wreath is 3" high.

Spoon seven small dots of remaining melted candy around top of wreath; press whole peppermints gently onto the wreath, allowing dots of melted candy to act as "glue." Let stand until firm. Decorate with bows, if desired. **Yield:** one 12" wreath.

*We used Golden Flake fat-free pretzels. You may want to buy two bags of pretzels just to be sure you get enough unbroken ones for the wreath.

Cinnamon-Nut-Caramel Apple Wreath

Autumn's smallest apples are costumed for Christmas in a sinful caramel and peanut butter dip, and then secured with cinnamon sticks and ribbon.

    3 tablespoons sugar
    1 teaspoon ground cinnamon
    2 tablespoons butter or margarine
    1 cup finely chopped peanuts
    ⅓ cup firmly packed dark brown sugar
    1 teaspoon ground cinnamon
   16 lady apples
       Kitchen shears
   16 long sticks cinnamon
    2 (14-ounce) packages caramels
    ¼ cup water
    ¼ cup creamy peanut butter
    ¼ cup peanut butter morsels
   16 (10") lengths of ribbon
   16 (4½") squares red cellophane or Mylar
    1 (18"-diameter) artificial pine wreath

Combine sugar and 1 teaspoon cinnamon in a small bowl; set aside.

Line a baking sheet with wax paper; lightly grease wax paper, and set aside.

Melt butter in a large skillet over medium heat. Add peanuts, brown sugar, and 1 teaspoon cinnamon. Cook over medium heat, stirring constantly, 4 minutes. Immediately spread peanut mixture onto prepared baking sheet; let cool. Break peanut candy mixture into small pieces, and place in a pieplate or other shallow container.

Line baking sheet with wax paper again; lightly grease wax paper, and set aside.

Wash and dry apples. If desired, cut cinnamon sticks down to 6", or leave them their original length. Make a hole in stem end of an apple with kitchen shears. Insert a cinnamon stick at least 1" into opening left by shears. Repeat procedure with remaining apples and cinnamon sticks.

Combine caramels and water in a large microwave-safe bowl. Microwave at HIGH 3 minutes or until caramels melt, stirring once. Stir in peanut butter and peanut butter morsels, stirring until morsels melt.

Dip apples into caramel mixture, covering completely. (Use a spoon to help with coating, if

necessary.) Sprinkle stem end of 8 apples with reserved cinnamon-sugar mixture. Roll bottom half of remaining 8 apples in reserved peanut candy mixture. Place apples on prepared baking sheet, allowing excess caramel to drip off; let cool. Chill apples 1 hour. Scrape off excess caramel with a knife, if desired.

Tie bows onto cinnamon sticks with ribbon. Place apples in lightly greased cellophane squares, and nestle into pine wreath. **Yield:** 16 apples.

Note: Your local craft store can supply you with the long cinnamon sticks, ribbon, cellophane, and wreath for this recipe. See Sources on page 154 for lady apples, or you can substitute small McIntosh or Jonathon apples.

COATING THE APPLES

◀ Make a hole in stem end of apples with kitchen shears. Insert cinnamon sticks at least 1" into apples.

◀ Dip apples into melted caramel, covering apples completely. Use a spoon to help with coating, if necessary.

◀ Roll bottoms of 8 apples in crushed peanut candy mixture.

Gingerbread Ring

    Snowy Icing, divided
 1 (12"-diameter) flat Styrofoam ring
 3 cups flaked coconut (about a 14-ounce bag)
    Gingerbread Men
12 (3") candy canes

Spread 1 tablespoon Snowy Icing on bottom of 12"
Styrofoam ring; place ring on a cake pedestal, frosting side down; press firmly. Frost top and sides of
ring with icing. Keep remaining icing covered with
a damp cloth. Sprinkle coconut over ring, pressing
gently with fingers.

  Spoon ½ teaspoon icing onto backs of each of 11
Gingerbread Men cookies. Press cookies against
outside of ring, working quickly. (Frosting dries
quickly.) Stand 13 cookies in a row on top of
wreath; stand 11 cookies in a row behind first row,
spacing them so heads show in both rows. Spoon ½
teaspoon icing onto backs of each of 10 cookies.
Press cookies against inside of ring.

  Press and stand 1 candy cane between each
cookie on outside of ring. To serve, use a small knife
to remove Gingerbread Men from ring, if necessary.
Yield: one 12" ring.

Snowy Icing

 4⅓ cups sifted powdered sugar
  3   tablespoons meringue powder
  ¼   cup plus 2 tablespoons water

Combine all ingredients in a large bowl. Beat at low
speed of an electric mixer until blended; beat at
medium speed 2 additional minutes. **Yield:** 3 cups.

Gingerbread Men

  ⅓ cup butter, softened
  ¾ cup firmly packed brown sugar
  1   large egg
  ½ cup molasses
 2¾ cups all-purpose flour
  ¾ teaspoon baking soda
  ½ teaspoon baking powder
  ¼ teaspoon salt
  2   teaspoons ground ginger
  ¾ teaspoon ground allspice
      Currants
      Red cinnamon candies, cut in half
      Candy-coated chewy fruit-flavored pieces*

Beat butter at medium speed of an electric mixer
until creamy; gradually add sugar, beating until
blended. Add egg, beating until blended. Add
molasses, beating well. Combine flour and next 5
ingredients; gradually add to molasses mixture, beating until blended. Cover and chill dough 2 hours.

  Roll half of dough to ¼" thickness on a floured
surface. Cut Gingerbread Men with a 3" cookie
cutter. Place on greased cookie sheets. Add excess
dough to remaining half of dough; wrap in wax
paper, and chill. Press currants, cinnamon candy
halves, and fruit-flavored candy pieces into cookies
for eyes, mouth, and buttons. Bake at 350° for 8
minutes or until lightly browned. Remove cookies to
wire racks; let cool completely. Repeat procedure
with remaining dough. **Yield:** about 4 dozen.

*For chewy fruit-flavored pieces, we used Skittles.
For Styrofoam ring, see Sources on page 154.

PREPARING GINGERBREAD AND FROSTING THE RING

▲Transfer Gingerbread dough
onto cookie sheet, using a pastry scraper or large spatula.

▲Cut cinnamon candies in half
easily with kitchen shears; use
them for Gingerbread mouths.

▲Frost Styrofoam ring.
Sprinkle with coconut,
and attach Gingerbread.

Stained Glass Holly Cake

Beneath this glistening edible artwork hides a moist white chocolate cake studded with cranberries and walnuts.

  1   cup butter, softened
  2   cups sugar
  5   large eggs
  1   cup sour cream
  ¼   teaspoon baking soda
  3   cups all-purpose flour
  4   (1-ounce) squares white chocolate, chopped*
  ½   cup dried cranberries
  ½   cup chopped walnuts, toasted
  ½   teaspoon vanilla extract
      White Glaze
  4   (.68- or .75-ounce) tubes green decorating gel
      Wooden picks
  1   (.68- or .75-ounce) tube black decorating gel
  1   (.68- or .75-ounce) tube red decorating gel

Beat butter at medium speed of an electric mixer 2 minutes or until creamy. Gradually add sugar, beating at medium speed 5 to 7 minutes. Add eggs, one at a time, beating just until yellow disappears.

Combine sour cream and soda. Add flour to butter mixture alternately with sour cream mixture, beginning and ending with flour. Beat at low speed just until blended after each addition. Stir in white chocolate and next 3 ingredients. Pour batter into a greased and floured 10" tube pan.

Bake at 325° for 1 hour and 15 minutes or until a wooden pick inserted in center comes out clean. Let cool in pan on a wire rack 10 to 15 minutes; remove from pan. Let cool completely on wire rack.

Line a jellyroll pan with wax paper; place under wire rack (to catch excess glaze). Working quickly, pour White Glaze over top of cake, pushing glaze down sides of cake with a spatula to cover cake completely. Let stand at least 1 hour. Transfer cake to a pedestal or other serving piece.

Using green gel, outline (freehand) leaves on top and sides of frosted cake. Add an additional small amount of green gel to center of each leaf; spread with wooden picks, filling in leaves completely.

Dot 1 end of each holly leaf with a small amount of black gel. Beginning at black dot at the base of each leaf, drag wooden pick down center; then drag wooden pick from center black line to tips of each leaf, creating veins. Using red gel, add 1 to 3 dots around base of each leaf to form holly berries. **Yield:** one 10" cake.

White Glaze

  6   (1-ounce) squares white chocolate, melted*
  3   tablespoons hot water
  1   teaspoon vanilla extract
  2   cups sifted powdered sugar

Combine chocolate, water, and vanilla in a bowl, stirring well. Gradually add powdered sugar, stirring until smooth. **Yield:** 1¼ cups.

*For white chocolate, we used Baker's.

Note: Find little tubes of decorating gel at the grocery store near the baking section. You'll be surprised how easy it is to draw these holly leaves.

DECORATING THE CAKE

◄ Draw the outlines of large holly leaves all over frosted cake. It takes several tubes of gel to cover cake.

◄ Spread gel with wooden picks, filling in leaves completely.

◄ Drag wooden picks through black gel to define the veins in leaves.

Assorted Appetizer Wreath

It makes a show-stopping first course, this ruffly wreath of hors d'oeuvres. You can make the recipe in four parts and prepare some of it up to two days ahead.

½ cup firmly packed brown sugar
½ cup soy sauce
½ cup rice vinegar
¼ cup minced fresh ginger
3 tablespoons dark sesame oil
2 (¾-pound) pork tenderloins
Vegetable cooking spray

12 spears fresh asparagus
1 tablespoon champagne mustard, divided*
12 very thin slices prosciutto ham (¼ pound)

2 dozen cherry tomatoes
2 ounces smoked salmon
5 ounces cream cheese, softened
1 teaspoon lemon juice

2 heads Belgian endive
2 tablespoons tomato chutney*
2 ounces roasted red peppers in a jar, drained and finely chopped (⅓ cup)
2 tablespoons feta cheese, finely crumbled

1 head green leaf lettuce
1 large head radicchio

Combine first 5 ingredients, stirring with a whisk until blended. Place pork in a large heavy-duty, zip-top plastic bag. Add brown sugar mixture; seal bag, and gently shake until pork is coated. Marinate in refrigerator 2 to 8 hours, turning bag often.

Remove pork from marinade, reserving marinade. Place marinade in a small saucepan, and bring to a boil. Remove from heat.

Coat grill rack with cooking spray; place on grill over medium-hot coals (350° to 400°). Place pork on rack; grill, covered, 20 minutes or until a meat thermometer inserted into thickest part of pork registers 160°, turning and basting twice with marinade. Let stand 10 minutes. Slice pork diagonally across the grain into thin slices; cover and chill.

Snap off tough ends of asparagus. Arrange asparagus in a steamer basket over boiling water;

Game Plan

TWO DAYS BEFORE PARTY:
•Prepare marinade for pork.

ONE DAY BEFORE PARTY:
•Marinate, grill, and slice pork tenderloins. Chill.
•Steam asparagus, and chill. Wrap asparagus with prosciutto.
•Prepare salmon mixture, and chill.
•Prepare tomato chutney mixture, and chill.

THE DAY OF PARTY:
•Stuff cherry tomatoes.
•Prepare endive leaves, and fill.
•Assemble wreath.

cover and steam 6 minutes or until crisp-tender. Plunge asparagus into ice water. Drain.

Spread ¼ teaspoon mustard on 1 side of each slice prosciutto. Wrap prosciutto, mustard side in, around asparagus. Cover and chill.

Cut top off each tomato; scoop out pulp, leaving shells intact. Discard pulp. Invert tomato shells onto paper towels to drain.

Position knife blade in food processor bowl; add salmon. Process 30 seconds. Add cream cheese and lemon juice. Process 1 minute or just until smooth. Spoon or pipe cream cheese mixture into tomato shells. Cover and chill.

Slice stem ends from endive, and separate leaves. Trim larger endive leaves to 3"; set aside. Combine chutney, red pepper, and feta cheese in a small bowl; stir well. Spoon mixture onto each endive leaf.

Line a large serving tray with leaf lettuce and radicchio, leaving a hole in center. Place asparagus spears, evenly spaced in spoke fashion, around lettuce wreath. Place 1 endive leaf between each asparagus spear. Fan pork slices above endive leaves. Place stuffed tomatoes above pork and in center of wreath. **Yield:** 12 servings.

*For champagne mustard, we used Old Spice. For tomato chutney, we used Alecia's. You can find these in jars, along with roasted red peppers, in specialty grocery stores on aisles with pickles and other condiments; or see Sources on page 154.

Note: If asparagus is not available, wrap green pepper strips or mozzarella cheese strips in prosciutto.

PREPARING THE WREATH

▲Slice and discard stem end from each head of endive; then separate the leaves.

▲Fan tenderloin slices above endive on the serving tray.

MAKING MEMORIES

Holidays are all about memories, and we offer you some terrific ways to fashion new ones. Create family traditions with an album to hold treasured mementos, fuzzy felt stockings to hang with care, or loads of ornaments for the tree.

Felt Star
Ornaments

Come deck the halls with the Brennans!

Join us for an
Ornament Exchange Party.

Festivities will begin at 5:30pm
December 6, 1996.

Please bring one ornament per person.
Regrets only 991-4031

Holiday Brunch
Menu

**Christmas
Memories Album**

Christmas
Memories

Christmas Memories Album

This handmade book is a beautiful way to store mementos of the season. Covered with wallpaper remnants and laced together with ribbon, it's an inexpensive alternative to similar albums found in specialty shops.

You will need:

diagrams on page 148 (optional)

¼" foam-core board: 2 (11½" x 1¼") pieces and 2 (11½" x 13¾") pieces (available at art supply stores)

sealing tape with filaments

12 sheets watercolor paper (available in tablets at art supply and craft stores)

deckle-edge scissors

broad-tip gold metallic opaque paint marker

metal-edge ruler

craft knife

craft glue

decorative envelopes (optional)

decorative metal corners (optional)

hole punch or awl

5' length wallpaper or desired decorative paper

metal title frame (optional)

large needle

2¼ yards ribbon

Note: If possible, have foam core cut when you purchase it. Mat cutting equipment makes a neater cut. For deckle-edge scissors, envelopes, decorative metal corners and frame, and wallpaper, see Sources on page 154. Finished album is shown on page 61.

1. To make album cover, place 1 narrow piece of foam-core board (11½" x 1¼") to the right of 1 large piece of foam-core board (11½" x 13¾"), aligning top and bottom edges. Place a pencil between pieces to maintain an even gap. Using sealing tape, tape 2 pieces together with 1 length of tape, taping from top to bottom of foam-core pieces and covering gap between pieces. Remove pencil. Turn foam-core unit

to underside. Place small pieces of tape across gap, taping down into gap and back up other side. This is the back cover.

Place remaining narrow piece of foam-core board to the left of remaining large foam-core piece. Place pencil between pieces to make uniform gap, and tape top and then underside in same manner as for back cover. This is the front cover.

2. To make pages, trim short outside edge of 10 sheets of watercolor paper with deckle-edge scissors. Draw paint marker along cut edge on front and back of sheets to create gold-edge pages.

To crease pages for easy opening, on opposite short edge of paper, use metal-edge ruler and blunt side of table knife to score a line parallel to and 1¼" from edge. Repeat, scoring a second line parallel to and 1½" from edge and a third line parallel to and 1¾" from edge. Gently fold paper first to 1 side and then to other along each scored line.

To make spacers, from 1 remaining sheet of watercolor paper, use ruler and craft knife to cut several 1½" x 11" strips to use as spacers. Place 3 or 4 spacers before each page with an envelope on it. By adding spacers, album will not bulge when closed. If necessary, cut more spacers from remaining watercolor paper to use before each page with envelopes. Also from watercolor paper, cut 1 piece to fit opening in decorative frame to be used as nameplate on album cover.

If desired, glue a decorative envelope at center of page. Glue decorative metal corners at bottom corners of envelope to embellish. When assembling album, remember to place 3 or 4 spacer strips in front of each envelope page.

Album Materials

3. To make holes in album and pages, with a hole punch or awl, make 5 evenly spaced holes in left edge of all pages and front and back covers, placing middle hole at center. If desired, create a template for a single page, and use it to ensure that all holes align. (For best alignment, have holes punched at a copy center.)

4. To cover album, using wallpaper or decorative paper, wrap paper to inside of front and back covers, folding paper at corners of cover for a mitered edge. Glue paper along edges. With scissors, clip paper at hinges. Glue a rectangle of wallpaper to inside cover,

concealing raw edges (see photo, above). Use a craft knife to cut holes in wallpaper at punched holes. If desired, place decorative metal frame on front cover of album. Glue on side and bottom edges, leaving top edge unglued. Write album title on card and slip into frame at top edge.

5. To bind album, place pages and spacers between covers. See diagrams on page 148 to lace as pictured on page 61. Or use a large needle, such as an upholstery or embroidery needle, to lace ribbon through holes as desired. Tie ends in bow.

Felt Filigree Tree Skirt

In Christmassy red and green, this traditional design has the punch of modern graphics. Fusible web makes quick work of the intricate-looking pattern.

You will need:
pattern and diagram on page 146
2 yards paper-backed fusible web
graph paper
36" square green felt
40" square red felt
rotary cutter or scissors
chalk
2 hooks and eyes (optional)

Note: Finished skirt is 36" in diameter. For felt, see Sources on page 154.

1. To make pattern, cut 2 (36") lengths of paper-backed fusible web and tape together lengthwise forming a 36" square. With a ruler and pencil, divide fusible web unit into 4 equal sections (see diagram). Using graph paper, enlarge skirt pattern. Trace pattern onto paper side of fusible web, transferring pattern onto each quarter, matching lines between sections.

2. To fuse felt pieces, following manufacturer's directions, fuse web to green felt. Cut out design along lines of traced pattern. Peel paper off back of green felt and center green felt piece on red felt. Following manufacturer's directions, fuse green felt piece to red felt.

3. To make opening for skirt, using a rotary cutter or scissors, cut opening for skirt through middle of 1 small design motif, cutting from edge of skirt to center of skirt.

4. To stitch pieces, beginning at skirt opening, stitch green felt design to red felt, stitching ⅛" in from edge of green felt. Stitch around entire green felt piece.

5. To trim outer edges, with ruler and chalk, measure and mark a cutting line 2" from outside edges of green felt design. Trim red felt along this line (see photo).

6. To cut center circle, cut a 4¼"-diameter circle from paper to use as a pattern. Pin paper circle to center of skirt and outline circle pattern with chalk. Cut out circle in center of skirt along marked line. To finish, close skirt with 2 hooks and eyes, or simply lap skirt at back to close.

Cyndi Wheeler of Birmingham, Alabama, uses her creative talents to relieve stress during the holidays. "As I make a gift for a friend, I take time to think of the lasting memories of that friendship. No longer do I feel hurried or pressured but thankful to be reminded of the true meaning of the season."

Star Power

Whimsical felt stars are the highlight of these simple-to-sew stockings and ornaments.

Felt Stocking

You will need (for 1 stocking):
patterns and diagrams on pages 150–151
tracing paper
24" x 36" medium-weight fusible interfacing
24" x 36" white felt
3 (4" x 6") felt rectangles, in 3 colors for stars
assorted buttons and bells
8-mm pearl cotton or metallic thread, to sew
    stocking and to add trims
embroidery needle

Note: For felt and buttons, see Sources on page 154.

1. To cut out stocking, trace pattern onto tracing paper, and extend lines at ankle 21¾" for stocking front and 14¾" for back. Cut 1 each front and back from interfacing and 1 each front and back from white felt. Following manufacturer's directions, fuse interfacing to inside of stocking pieces, leaving top 7" of front free of interfacing. (Top 7" folds forward to form cuff.)

2. To add stars, using pattern, cut stars from 3 colors of felt. Position bottom 2 stars on front stocking piece as shown in photo. (*Note:* Top star is added to cuff after it has been folded forward.) Sew button in center of each star to secure. Fold cuff forward. Sew bottom half of top star to cuff with running stitch. Trim cuff to match star shape along bottom edges (see Diagram 1).

3. To add buttons, on stocking front, with pencil, lightly draw heel and toe patterns and candy stripe lines on stocking (see Diagram 2). Sew buttons and bells on heel, toe, and stripes.

4. To finish, with wrong sides together and raw edges aligned, sew stocking front and back together with running stitch. Sew ½" x 5" felt loop between layers at top back edge of stocking for hanging.

Felt Star Ornament

You will need (for 1 ornament):
pattern on page 151
tracing paper
2 (4" x 6") rectangles fusible interfacing
2 (4" x 6") felt rectangles
8-mm pearl cotton or metallic thread, to sew
    ornament and to add trims
embroidery needle
assorted buttons
    and bells

To make ornament, using pattern, cut 2 stars from interfacing and 2 stars from felt. Trim interfacing ⅛" on all sides. Following manufacturer's directions, fuse interfacing to back of each felt star. With wrong sides facing, sew front and back pieces together with running stitch. Sew on buttons and bells, as desired. Add 6" thread loop at top for hanging.

Note: For directions to make tassels, see page 151.

Swirly Spirals for the Tree

These playful twists add spirited fun to traditional trimmings.
They're also terrific package toppers.

You will need:
rubber gloves
craft clay: dark brown, maroon (Sculpey III used)
wax metallic finish: gold, silver (Rub 'n Buff used)
stiff-bristled paintbrush
ribbon, cord, wire, or thread for hanging

Note: For each ornament, use ½ package Sculpey. For craft clay, see Sources on page 154.

1. To shape each ornament, roll clay into ball. Wear rubber gloves while handling clay to prevent transferring fingerprints. Form ball into ¼"-wide and 15"-long log. Taper ends, if desired. Referring to photo, form log into desired shape on baking sheet. Don't worry about mistakes; craft clay can be remolded easily before baking. Using sharp knife, trim excess clay. To form tight spiral, wrap log around wooden spoon handle to bake. Press clay to flatten outer curves and ends. Stretching out shapes produces interesting variations. Use toothpick or small nail to form hole for hanging.

2. To bake, place ornaments in oven and bake at 275° for about 20 minutes. Let cool for 20 minutes.

3. To paint, with stiff paintbrush, apply finish to ornaments, allowing some clay color to show through. With gloved finger, apply thicker layers of finish in random fashion on ornament, if desired. (*Note:* Finish dries very quickly and will not rub off.)

For hanger, use ribbon, cord, wire, or thread.

Claudia Williams of Nashville, Tennessee, treasures the fond recollections Christmas ornaments bring. Her unusual clay designs can be displayed hanging from a ribbon on a lamp or in a window as a year-round expression of friendship.

Framed in Gold

Glue on the charm and capture a memory in a frame
that's a snap to make.

You will need:
diagrams on page 144
2 (5" x 5") pieces foam-core board
craft knife
gold metallic spray paint
spray adhesive
40 (approximately) brass- or gold-colored
  assorted charms
thick craft glue

Note: For charms, see Sources on page 154.

1. To cut opening for photo, mark center point
of 1 piece of foam-core board. Measure and mark 1"
from center vertically and horizontally. Connect
marks to create a 2" square in center of foam-core
piece. Using ruler as your straight edge, carefully
score marked lines with craft knife on each side of
square until you have completely cut out center.

2. To make frame stand, referring to diagram, on
remaining piece of foam-core board, draw a line
extending 3½" up from center bottom. Using a ruler,
start at top point of line and draw a diagonal line

ending at bottom of foam-core board. Using craft
knife, carefully cut midway through foam-core board
on vertical fold line. (*Note:* Do not cut through completely.) On diagonal line, using ruler as your
straight edge, score line with craft knife until you
have cut through board completely. Trim bottom of
stand as indicated on diagram. Gently fold stand out.

With gold metallic spray paint, paint outsides and
edges of frame front, back, and stand, covering completely. Let dry.

3. To assemble frame, with spray adhesive, on
unpainted side of frame front, coat top horizontal
side and ⅓ down both vertical sides. (*Note:* Unglued
portion at frame bottom provides opening for
photo.) Position frame back, unpainted side down,
on top of unpainted side of frame front, aligning
edges. With fingers, press front and back pieces
together to secure. Frame stand bends to outside
back of frame.

4. To decorate frame, glue assorted charms
around picture opening on front of frame. Layer
charms, letting glue dry between each layer.

Trinket Box Ornaments

These gift packages are right at home on the tree. Tuck a tiny treasure into each one for a Christmas morning surprise.

Note: For stickers, see Sources on page 154.

Use your imagination and materials you have on hand to create diminutive ornaments. Start with **small jewelry boxes or papier-mâché boxes** found at craft stores. Paint boxes with **acrylic paint** or wrap them with **decorative paper or fabric.** Then glue on **ribbon** and **braid,** or use **stickers, beads, or bells** to embellish.

    To make a hanger, fold a 6" to 8" length of ⅛"-diameter **cording** in half, and knot the ends

together twice, making 1 large knot. Pierce a hole in the center of each box lid. Pull the hanger through the hole. The knot will keep the hanger from pulling through. Apply a small drop of glue to the underside of the lid, if desired. Attach **tassels** in the same way, piercing a hole in the bottom of each box.

    To finish, hot-glue the top and the bottom of the box together to secure.

For **Dondra Parham** of Alpharetta, Georgia, unwrapping the ornaments for the tree is really an unveiling of many wonderful memories. As she says, "We add ornaments to our collection to mark special events, and the holiday mementos we receive from friends always bring a smile."

BEYOND THE BASIC SUGAR COOKIE

Dressing sugar cookie dough in red and green is a timeless Christmas tradition. Turn the page, and this cherished cookie is transformed into other unexpected and delightful desserts.

Cinnamon-Sugar Fig Tart

Sugar Cookie Torte

Sugar Crinkles and Rolled
Cinnamon-Sugar Angels

Vanilla Sugar
Loaf

Cinnamon-Sugar
Fig Tart

Sugar Crinkles

Brown Sugar Cookies

Sugar Crinkles

Your kitchen will smell like a bakery when you make these tender treasures. For burlap packaging, see Sources on page 154.

> 1 cup shortening
> 1½ cups sugar
> 2 large eggs
> 1 teaspoon lemon extract
> 1 teaspoon vanilla extract
> 2½ cups all-purpose flour
> 2 teaspoons baking powder
> ½ teaspoon salt
> ¼ cup sugar

Beat shortening and 1½ cups sugar at medium speed of an electric mixer until fluffy. Add eggs and flavorings, beating until blended.

Combine flour, baking powder, and salt; gradually add to shortening mixture, beating well. Cover and chill dough.

Shape dough into 1" balls. Roll balls in ¼ cup sugar. Place balls on ungreased cookie sheets.

Bake at 350° for 8 to 9 minutes or until barely golden. Let cool 2 minutes on cookie sheets. Remove to wire racks to cool completely. **Yield:** about 5½ dozen.

Brown Sugar Cookies

When real butter and dark brown sugar blend and bake, you get these crisp praline-tasting cookies.

> 1 cup butter, softened
> 1½ cups firmly packed dark brown sugar
> 1 large egg
> 1 teaspoon vanilla extract
> 3⅓ cups all-purpose flour
> 1 teaspoon baking soda
> ½ teaspoon salt
>   Decorator sugar

Beat butter at medium speed of an electric mixer until creamy. Gradually add brown sugar, beating well. Add egg and vanilla, beating well.

Combine flour, soda, and salt; add to butter mixture, beating just until blended.

Roll dough to ¼" thickness between two sheets of wax paper. Cut with 4" cookie cutters. Place 1" apart on ungreased cookie sheets. Sprinkle cookies with decorator sugar.

Bake at 350° for 10 to 12 minutes. Let cookies cool 1 minute on cookie sheets, and carefully transfer to wire racks to cool completely. **Yield:** about 2½ dozen.

Sugar Cookie Cran-Apple Cobbler

Borrow some Brown Sugar Cookie dough (left) for this cobbler's crust.

2 cups fresh or frozen cranberries
1½ cups sugar
⅔ cup water
5 large cooking apples, peeled and chopped
2 tablespoons cornstarch
2 tablespoons water
1 cup coarsely chopped pecans
½ cup raisins
½ recipe Brown Sugar Cookie dough
  Vanilla ice cream (optional)

Combine first 4 ingredients in a Dutch oven or large saucepan; bring to a boil. Cover, reduce heat, and simmer 10 minutes.

Combine cornstarch and 2 tablespoons water, stirring mixture until smooth. Add to cranberry mixture, stirring well. Bring to a boil; reduce heat, and simmer, uncovered, until thickened. Remove from heat; stir in pecans and raisins. Spoon mixture into a lightly greased 11" x 7" x 1½" baking dish.

Flatten Brown Sugar Cookie dough into a disc, and place between two sheets of wax paper on a large cutting board. Roll dough into a 10" square. Chill 10 minutes.

Cut dough into 14 strips, using a pastry wheel or knife. Arrange strips diagonally in a lattice design over fruit mixture. Trim excess dough.

Bake, uncovered, at 350° for 30 minutes or until filling is bubbly and cookie topping is done. Let cobbler cool 10 minutes on a wire rack. Spoon into individual bowls; top with ice cream, if desired. **Yield**: 8 servings.

Sugar Cookie Cran-Apple Cobbler

Rolled Cinnamon-Sugar Angels

This tender cinnamon dough deserves its celestial shape, but works fine with whatever cutters you have on hand.

- ¾ cup unsalted butter, softened
- 1 cup sugar
- 1 large egg
- 1 teaspoon vanilla extract
- 3 cups all-purpose flour
- 2 teaspoons baking powder
- ½ teaspoon baking soda
- ½ teaspoon ground cinnamon
- ¼ teaspoon salt
- 1 (15-ounce) container creamy vanilla frosting

Beat butter at medium speed of an electric mixer until fluffy; gradually add sugar, beating well. Add egg and vanilla, beating well. Combine flour and next 4 ingredients; gradually add to butter mixture, beating until blended. Shape dough into a ball. Cover and chill 30 minutes.

Roll dough to ⅛" thickness on a lightly floured surface. Cut with a 3" angel-shaped cookie cutter, and gently transfer to lightly greased cookie sheets (dough is fragile). Bake at 375° for 6 to 7 minutes or until lightly browned. Carefully remove cookies to wire racks to cool. Place frosting in a microwave-safe bowl. Microwave, uncovered, at HIGH 45 seconds or just until pourable; spoon frosting on top of cookies. Let stand on wire racks until dry. **Yield:** 3 dozen.

Cinnamon-Sugar Fig Tarts

These delicate desserts use the cinnamon-sugar cookie dough at left.

- 1 recipe Rolled Cinnamon-Sugar Angels dough
- 1 (10.5- or 11-ounce) jar fig preserves*
- ½ cup chopped pitted dates
- ½ cup chopped walnuts or pecans, toasted
- 2 tablespoons brown sugar
- ¼ teaspoon ground allspice

Roll dough to ¼" thickness on a lightly floured surface. Cut and fit dough into nine lightly greased 3" tart pans, reserving dough scraps.

Combine preserves and remaining 4 ingredients; stir well. Spoon filling mixture into tart pans.

Roll dough scraps to ⅛" thickness; cut half of dough into ¼" strips. Cut remaining half of dough with small cookie cutters.

Arrange strips of dough, lattice fashion, across tops of 4 tarts. Place shaped cutouts on tops of remaining tarts. (Reserve any remaining dough, and bake according to directions for Rolled Cinnamon-Sugar Angels at left.)

Place tarts on a baking sheet. Bake at 375° for 15 minutes or until golden. Let cool on a wire rack. Gently remove from pans. **Yield:** 9 tarts.

*For fig preserves, we used Braswell's.

Rolled Cinnamon-Sugar Angels

Cinnamon-Sugar
Fig Tarts

Vanilla
Sugar Loaf

Vanilla Sugar Loaf

It's the tiny seeds inside the bean that tell of vanilla's essence. Use the seeds to make vanilla sugar in this simple buttery cake, which also absorbs a vanilla glaze.

> 1¼ cups sugar
> 1 whole vanilla bean
> 2 cups plus 2 tablespoons sifted cake flour
> 1 teaspoon baking powder
> ½ teaspoon salt
> 1 cup unsalted butter, softened
> 4 large eggs
> ⅓ cup sifted powdered sugar
> 1 tablespoon milk
> 1 teaspoon vanilla extract

Pour 1¼ cups sugar into a jar. Split vanilla bean in half lengthwise. Scrape tiny vanilla bean seeds into sugar; cut bean into 1" pieces, and add to vanilla sugar. Cover and shake vigorously to mix, or stir well. Let stand 24 hours.

Combine flour, baking powder, and salt; stir well. Beat butter at low speed of an electric mixer until creamy. Remove and discard pieces of vanilla bean from sugar. Gradually add vanilla sugar to butter, beating at medium speed until light and fluffy. Add eggs, one at a time, beating well after each addition. Gradually add flour mixture to butter mixture, beating at low speed just until blended.

Pour batter into a lightly greased and floured 9" x 5" x 3" loafpan. Bake at 325° for 1 hour or until a wooden pick inserted in center comes out clean. Let cool in pan on a wire rack 15 minutes.

Meanwhile, combine powdered sugar, milk, and vanilla extract; stir well. Prick tiny holes in top of loaf with a wooden pick. Spoon glaze mixture over warm loaf; let cool in pan on a wire rack 15 additional minutes. Remove from pan, and let cool completely on a wire rack. **Yield:** 1 loaf.

Note: Don't be intimidated by vanilla beans. Find them as leathery brown beans folded in a narrow glass tube or bottle on the spice aisle.

▲Split vanilla bean in half lengthwise, using a small sharp knife.

▲Scrape tiny seeds out with tip of knife.

Sugar Cookie Torte

Sugar cookie crumbs replace most of the flour in this dense, bumpy textured, and very buttery European-style torte. It needs no adornment—only a sip of espresso.

- 2 **cups slivered almonds, toasted**
- 1 **cup unsalted butter, softened**
- 2 **cups sugar**
- 6 **large eggs**
- 2 **(5¼-ounce) packages sugar cookies, finely crushed (3 cups)***
- ½ **cup all-purpose flour**
- ⅓ **cup half-and-half**
- 1½ **tablespoons vanilla extract**
  Powdered sugar (optional)

Draw a 10" circle on a piece of wax paper, using a 10" tube pan as a guide. Cut out circle. Set tube pan insert in center of circle, and draw around inside of tube; cut out smaller circle. Grease bottom of pan, and line with wax paper cutout; heavily grease and flour wax paper and sides of pan. Set aside.

Position knife blade in food processor bowl; add almonds. Pulse 4 to 5 times or until almonds are coarsely ground. (Be careful not to overprocess, as this releases oil from the almonds.)

Beat butter at medium speed of an electric mixer until creamy; gradually add 2 cups sugar, beating well. Add eggs, one at a time, beating after each addition. Combine cookie crumbs and flour; add to butter mixture alternately with half-and-half, beginning and ending with crumb mixture. Beat at low speed just until blended after each addition. Stir in ground almonds and vanilla.

Spoon batter into prepared pan. (Batter will fill pan only half full.) Bake at 300° for 1 hour and 40 minutes or until a wooden pick inserted in center comes out clean. (Torte rises only slightly.) Let cool completely in pan on a wire rack.

Run a sharp knife around edge of pan to loosen torte. Carefully invert torte onto a serving plate; peel off wax paper. Invert torte again. Sift powdered sugar over torte, if desired. **Yield:** one 10" torte.

*We used Pepperidge Farm sugar cookies, but other brands of sugar cookies would work as well in this torte.

Sugar Cookie Torte

Cranberry Swirl Cheesecake
with Sugar Cookie Crust

Cranberry Swirl Cheesecake with Sugar Cookie Crust

Our test kitchen staff discovered that Pepperidge Farm Bordeaux cookies make a great crumb crust. See the box at right for other crust discoveries.

2¼ cups Bordeaux cookie crumbs
¼ cup butter or margarine, melted
1 (16-ounce) can whole-berry cranberry sauce
2 teaspoons ground cinnamon
¼ teaspoon ground cloves
3 (8-ounce) packages cream cheese, softened
1 cup sugar
1 tablespoon cornstarch
4 large eggs
1 teaspoon vanilla extract
   Garnishes: sweetened whipped cream, fresh cranberries, fresh mint

Combine cookie crumbs and melted butter; stir well. Press crumb mixture onto bottom and 1" up sides of a lightly greased 9" springform pan. Bake at 350° for 10 minutes. Let crust cool completely on a wire rack.

Position knife blade in food processor bowl. Add cranberry sauce and spices; process until smooth. Set aside.

Beat cream cheese at medium speed of an electric mixer until smooth. Add sugar and cornstarch; beat well. Add eggs, one at a time, beating just until blended after each addition. Stir in vanilla.

Pour half of batter into cookie crust; spoon ½ cup cranberry mixture over batter. Swirl gently with a knife. Top with remaining batter. Spoon ½ cup cranberry mixture over cheesecake, and swirl gently with a knife.

Bake at 350° for 15 minutes. Reduce oven temperature to 225°. Bake 1 hour and 10 minutes.

Remove from oven, and immediately run a knife around sides of cheesecake to loosen it from pan. Turn oven off; return cheesecake to oven, and let cool in oven 1 hour. Remove from oven; let cool completely in pan on a wire rack. Chill, uncovered, until ready to serve. (Cheesecake will continue to firm up as it chills.)

Remove sides of pan. Garnish, if desired. Serve cheesecake with remaining cranberry mixture, if desired. **Yield**: one 9" cheesecake.

Crust Conversions

Calling all cheesecake aficionados. Do you have a favorite cheesecake recipe? How about making a minor change so it seems brand new? Here are some suggestions for cookies and crackers that make great cheesecake crusts.

- Instead of using regular graham crackers for a crumb crust, try cinnamon graham crackers, vanilla wafers, saltine crackers, round buttery crackers (Ritz), thin pretzel sticks, or wheat-meal biscuits (Carr's).
- Rather than using chocolate wafers (Nabisco) for a crumb crust, try chocolate graham crackers or chocolate teddy bear-shaped cookies.
- Other crust options are pecan shortbread cookies (Pecan Sandies), commercial crisp sugar cookies, or thin gingersnaps.

Just remember this rule of thumb: Choose a cookie that has a similar texture to the original. Don't alter the other crust ingredients like butter or chopped nuts unless the cookie you choose is especially buttery; then you may want to reduce butter in crust by 1 to 2 tablespoons.

CHOCOLATE CRAVINGS

Little Chocolate-
Kahlúa Fruitcakes

Speckled Biscotti

Heavenly Chocolate Chunk Cookies

Mint Chocolate Crumble Bars

Caramel Fudge Cutouts

Spicy Cocoa Snaps

Peanut Butter and Chocolate Truffle Torte

A chocolate lover's dream awaits. If you desire the decadent dark sweet stuff, indulge in these recipes that use almost every kind of chocolate.

Speckled Biscotti

Speckled Biscotti

The speckles are sweet in these twice-baked Italian cookies. And because biscotti are crunchy by nature, they benefit from a dip in your coffee.

  4½ cups all-purpose flour
   1   teaspoon baking powder
  ½   teaspoon baking soda
  ½   teaspoon salt
  1½ cups sugar
  ⅔   cup vegetable oil
   2   large eggs
  ½   cup sour cream
  ½   cup chopped pecans, toasted
  ½   cup semisweet chocolate morsels
   1   (3-ounce) package dried cranberries
        (about ½ cup)
   1   egg yolk
   2   teaspoons water
        Additional sugar

Combine first 4 ingredients; stir well. Combine sugar, oil, and eggs; beat at medium speed of a heavy-duty electric mixer until blended. Gradually add flour mixture alternately with sour cream, beginning and ending with flour mixture. Gently stir or knead in pecans, chocolate morsels, and cranberries.

Turn dough out onto a lightly floured surface. Divide dough into 3 portions. Shape each portion into a 14" log; place logs several inches apart on a lightly greased large cookie sheet. Combine egg yolk and water; brush lightly over each log. Sprinkle each log with additional sugar.

Bake at 350° for 30 minutes. Let logs cool 30 minutes on cookie sheet. (This will make slicing easier.) Transfer logs to a cutting board, and cut diagonally into ¾" slices. Place slices on two ungreased cookie sheets. Reduce oven temperature to 300°. Bake at 300° for 15 to 20 minutes or just until firm. Let cool completely on wire racks. Store in an airtight container up to 1 week, or freeze up to 1 month. **Yield:** 4½ dozen.

Note: If you don't own a heavy-duty mixer, you can use a hand-held mixer until it's time to add flour; then you'll probably have to stir the last 2 cups of flour in by hand with a sturdy spoon.

Tiger Cookies

Ribbons of melted milk chocolate swirl through these crunchy little cookies.

- ³⁄₄ cup butter-flavored shortening
- 1 cup firmly packed brown sugar
- 2 large eggs
- 1 teaspoon vanilla extract
- 2 cups all-purpose flour
- 1 teaspoon baking powder
- ¹⁄₂ teaspoon salt
- ¹⁄₂ teaspoon ground cinnamon
- 3 cups sugar-coated corn flakes cereal, slightly crushed
- 1 cup (6 ounces) milk chocolate morsels, melted and cooled to room temperature

Beat shortening in a large mixing bowl at medium speed of an electric mixer until creamy. Gradually add sugar, beating until blended. Add eggs, one at a time, beating well after each addition. Stir in vanilla.

Combine flour and next 3 ingredients; stir well. Add to sugar mixture, blending well. Stir in cereal.

Drizzle half of chocolate over dough; stir lightly. Drizzle remaining chocolate over dough; stir lightly, leaving streaks of chocolate. Drop dough by heaping teaspoonfuls 2" apart onto ungreased cookie sheets. Bake at 350° for 8 to 10 minutes or until golden. Remove to wire racks to cool. **Yield:** about 5 dozen.

Chewy Brownie Grahams

You won't believe these fudgy-chewy brownies have only five ingredients and still received the highest test kitchen rating. The thick batter is loaded with chocolate cookie crumbs.

- 1 cup (6 ounces) semisweet chocolate morsels
- ¹⁄₂ cup creamy or chunky peanut butter
- 1 (14-ounce) can sweetened condensed milk
- ¹⁄₂ cup coarsely chopped pecans, toasted
- 2 cups chocolate graham cracker crumbs or chocolate wafer cookie crumbs

Combine first 3 ingredients in a saucepan; cook over medium heat, stirring constantly, until morsels and peanut butter melt. Remove from heat. Stir in pecans and chocolate crumbs. (Batter will be very thick.) Press batter into a heavily greased 8" square pan. Bake at 350° for 24 minutes. Let cool in pan. Cut into 2" squares. **Yield:** 16 brownies.

Spicy Cocoa Snaps

Dark rum and coriander add a surprising Caribbean flair to these slice-and-bake cookies.

- 1¹⁄₂ cups all-purpose flour
- ³⁄₄ cup cocoa
- 1 teaspoon ground cinnamon
- ¹⁄₄ teaspoon salt
- ¹⁄₄ teaspoon ground coriander
- ¹⁄₄ teaspoon ground nutmeg
- ¹⁄₄ teaspoon ground cloves
- ¹⁄₈ teaspoon pepper
- ³⁄₄ cup butter, softened
- 1 cup sugar
- 1 large egg
- 2 tablespoons dark rum

Combine first 8 ingredients; stir well. Beat butter in a large bowl at medium speed of an electric mixer until creamy; gradually add sugar, beating well. Add egg, beating until blended. Stir in rum. Gradually add flour mixture, beating just until blended after each addition. Cover and chill dough 45 minutes.

Shape dough into a 13" log on wax paper; wrap and freeze log 1 hour or until firm.

Cut frozen log into ¹⁄₄" slices, and place on lightly greased cookie sheets. Bake at 350° for 12 minutes. Remove to wire racks to cool completely. **Yield:** about 4 dozen.

Spicy Cocoa Snaps

Heavenly Chocolate Chunk Cookies

Mega-morsels give a big chocolate taste to every bite of these deluxe chocolate chip cookies.

 2 cups plus 2 tablespoons all-purpose flour
 ½ teaspoon baking soda
 ½ teaspoon salt
 ¾ cup butter or margarine
 2 tablespoons instant coffee granules
 1 cup firmly packed brown sugar
 ½ cup sugar
 1 large egg
 1 egg yolk
 1 (11.5-ounce) package semisweet chocolate mega-morsels
 1 cup walnut halves, toasted

Combine first 3 ingredients; stir well.

Combine butter and coffee granules in a small saucepan or skillet. Cook over medium-low heat until butter melts and coffee granules dissolve, stirring occasionally. Remove from heat, and let cool to room temperature (don't let butter resolidify).

Combine butter mixture, sugars, egg, and egg yolk in a large bowl. Beat at medium speed of an electric mixer until blended. Gradually add flour mixture, beating at low speed just until blended. Stir in mega-morsels and walnuts.

Drop dough by heaping tablespoonfuls 2" apart onto ungreased cookie sheets. Bake at 325° for 12 to 14 minutes. Let cool slightly on cookie sheets. Remove to wire racks to cool completely. **Yield:** 20 cookies.

Heavenly
Chocolate Chunk
Cookies

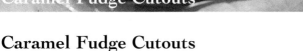

Caramel Fudge Cutouts

Mint Chocolate
Crumble Bars

Caramel Fudge Cutouts

- 2　cups sugar
- ¼　cup cocoa
- ¾　cup milk
- 2　tablespoons light corn syrup
- ¼　cup plus 2 tablespoons butter, divided
- 8　caramels, chopped
- ¾　cup chopped skinned hazelnuts or pecans
- 2　teaspoons vanilla extract

Line a 9" square pan with aluminum foil, allowing foil to extend over edges of pan. Butter foil, and set aside.

Butter insides of a heavy 3-quart saucepan. Combine sugar and cocoa in saucepan, stirring well. Stir in milk and corn syrup. Bring to a boil over medium-low heat, stirring gently and constantly with a wooden spoon, until sugar dissolves (6 to 8 minutes). Add ¼ cup butter, stirring until butter melts. Cover and boil 3 minutes over medium heat.

Uncover and cook, without stirring, until candy thermometer registers 238° (about 14 minutes). Remove from heat. Add remaining 2 tablespoons butter, chopped caramels, nuts, and vanilla. Do not stir. Let mixture cool to 130° (about 25 minutes).

Beat fudge by hand with a wooden spoon until it thickens and begins to lose its gloss (10 minutes). Quickly spread fudge into prepared pan; let cool (about 3 hours). Lift uncut fudge out of pan with foil; discard foil, and place fudge on a cutting board. Cut desired shapes, using 2" cookie cutters, or cut fudge into 1½" squares. **Yield:** 16 cutouts or 3 dozen squares.

Mint Chocolate Crumble Bars

- 1　(10-ounce) package teddy bear-shaped chocolate graham cracker cookies, crushed (about 2½ cups)
- ½　cup butter or margarine, melted
- 3　(1.55-ounce) minty milk chocolate bars with crunchy cookie bits, chopped*
- 6　(1-ounce) squares white baking bar or white chocolate, chopped*
- 1　cup chopped pistachios or pecans
- 1　cup flaked coconut
- 1　cup (6 ounces) semisweet chocolate morsels
- 1　large egg, lightly beaten
- 1　(14-ounce) can sweetened condensed milk

Combine cookie crumbs and melted butter; stir well. Press into a lightly greased 13" x 9" x 2" pan. Bake at 350° for 15 minutes.

Sprinkle chopped candy bars and next 4 ingredients over crust. Combine egg and condensed milk; pour over chocolate morsels.

Bake at 350° for 35 minutes. Let cool completely. Cut into bars. **Yield:** 2½ dozen.

*For candy bars, we used Hershey's Cookies 'n' Mint bars. For white chocolate, we used Baker's.

Black and White Cheesecake

Black and White Cheesecake

Big chips of coconut spike the soft whipped cream that covers this dark cheesecake.

1½	cups shortbread cookie crumbs
2	tablespoons sugar
3	tablespoons butter or margarine, melted
¾	cup butter or margarine
8	(1-ounce) squares semisweet chocolate
1	(8-ounce) package cream cheese, softened
1	(3-ounce) package cream cheese, softened
½	cup sugar
3	large eggs
⅓	cup cream of coconut
1¼	cups whipping cream
2	tablespoons powdered sugar
½	teaspoon vanilla extract
1	(3-ounce) package coconut chips*

Combine first 3 ingredients; stir well. Press into bottom of a greased 9" springform pan. Bake at 350° for 10 to 12 minutes or until toasted. Remove from oven, and reduce oven temperature to 300°.

Combine ¾ cup butter and chocolate in a heavy saucepan. Cook over medium-low heat until melted, stirring often. Remove from heat, and let cool.

Beat cream cheese at medium speed of an electric mixer until creamy. Add ½ cup sugar; beat well. Add eggs, one at a time, beating just until blended after each addition. Stir in cooled chocolate mixture and cream of coconut. Pour over crust in pan. Bake at 300° for 40 minutes or until cheesecake is barely set. Let cool to room temperature in pan on a wire rack; cover and chill 8 hours.

Beat whipping cream at high speed until foamy; gradually add powdered sugar, beating until soft peaks form. Add vanilla; beat just until blended.

Carefully remove sides of springform pan. Place cheesecake on serving plate. Frost top and sides with whipped cream mixture. Gently press coconut onto sides, and sprinkle on top of frosted cheesecake. Chill thoroughly. **Yield:** one 9" cheesecake.

*For coconut chips, we used Melissa's. You can find them near packets of dried fruits in grocery stores; you can also buy these fat coconut shavings in stores where nuts are sold in bulk. Or you can substitute flaked coconut.

Little Chocolate-Kahlúa Fruitcakes

This fruitcake recipe is like none other. It's gooey and brownielike and unforgettable.

Little Chocolate-Kahlúa Fruitcakes

1   cup butter
6   (1-ounce) squares semisweet chocolate
1   teaspoon instant coffee granules
1   cup firmly packed brown sugar
3   large eggs, separated
¼ cup plus 2 tablespoons Kahlúa or other coffee-flavored liqueur, divided
1   teaspoon vanilla extract
2   cups all-purpose flour, divided
½ teaspoon baking soda
¼ teaspoon salt
1   (10-ounce) container whole pitted dates, chopped (about 1¾ cups)
1½ cups chopped pecans, toasted
1   cup semisweet chocolate mega-morsels or regular morsels
¾ cup dried apricots, chopped
    Additional Kahlúa

Grease five 6" x 3" x 2" loafpans. Line bottoms of loafpans with wax paper; set aside.

Melt butter and chocolate in a heavy saucepan over low heat, stirring often. Stir in coffee granules. Remove mixture from heat, and let cool 15 minutes. Pour into a large bowl. Stir in brown sugar. Add egg yolks, stirring well. Add 2 tablespoons Kahlúa and vanilla; stir well.

Combine 1½ cups flour, soda, and salt; add to chocolate mixture. Combine dates and next 3 ingredients; sprinkle with remaining ½ cup flour, tossing to coat. Stir fruit mixture into batter. Beat egg whites at high speed of an electric mixer until stiff peaks form; fold into batter.

Spoon batter evenly into prepared pans. Bake at 300° for 1 hour and 15 minutes or until a wooden pick inserted in center comes out clean. Let cool in pans on a wire rack 10 minutes; remove from pans, and brush loaves with remaining ¼ cup Kahlúa. Let cool completely on a wire rack.

Wrap fruitcakes in Kahlúa-soaked cheesecloth. Store in an airtight container in a cool place at least 1 week before serving. Pour a small amount of Kahlúa over each loaf every week up to 1 month. To serve, slice with an electric knife. **Yield:** 5 loaves.

Chocolate-Orange Cream Cake

Here's a fancy chocolate cake for sure, smothered in a swirly blanket of thick frosting.

½ cup Dutch process cocoa*
½ cup boiling water
⅔ cup shortening
1¾ cups sugar
4 large eggs
1½ cups buttermilk
1½ teaspoons baking soda
¼ teaspoon salt
2½ cups all-purpose flour
1 teaspoon orange extract
  Cream Filling
  Grand Marnier Frosting
  Garnishes: orange slices and curls,
  chocolate ribbons

Grease three 8" round cakepans; line with wax paper. Grease and flour wax paper and sides of pans. Set aside.

Combine cocoa and boiling water in a small bowl; stir until smooth. Set aside.

Beat shortening at medium speed of an electric mixer until creamy; gradually add sugar, beating until light and fluffy (about 5 minutes). Add eggs, one at a time, beating after each addition.

Combine buttermilk, soda, and salt. Add flour to shortening mixture alternately with buttermilk mixture, beginning and ending with flour. Beat at low speed after each addition until blended. Stir in cocoa mixture and orange extract. Beat 2 additional minutes.

Pour batter into prepared pans. Bake at 350° for 25 minutes or until a wooden pick inserted in center comes out clean. Let cake layers cool in pans 10 minutes; remove from pans. Peel off wax paper, and let layers cool completely on wire racks.

Spread Cream Filling between layers to within ½" of edge. Spread Grand Marnier Frosting on sides and top of cake. Garnish, if desired. **Yield:** one 3-layer cake.

*We prefer a dutched cocoa such as Droste or Hershey's European-style in the cake layers for the richest flavor (but the recipe will still taste good if you use Hershey's non-alkalized natural cocoa).

Cream Filling

2 tablespoons all-purpose flour
¼ cup plus 1 tablespoon milk
¼ cup shortening
2 tablespoons butter or margarine, softened
½ teaspoon orange extract
⅛ teaspoon salt
2 cups sifted powdered sugar

Combine flour and milk in a small saucepan; cook over low heat, stirring constantly with a wire whisk, 3 minutes or until mixture resembles a soft frosting and is thick enough to hold its shape. (Do not boil.) Remove from heat; let cool.

Beat shortening and butter at medium speed of an electric mixer until creamy; add flour mixture, orange extract, and salt, beating well. Gradually add sugar, beating at high speed 4 to 5 minutes or until fluffy. **Yield:** 1½ cups.

Grand Marnier Frosting

½ cup butter, softened
3 (1-ounce) squares unsweetened chocolate, melted
¼ cup Grand Marnier (orange liqueur) or orange juice*
¼ cup whipping cream
1 (16-ounce) package powdered sugar, sifted

Beat butter at medium speed of an electric mixer until creamy. Add chocolate, Grand Marnier, and whipping cream; beat well. Gradually add sugar, beating at high speed 5 minutes or until spreading consistency. **Yield:** 3 cups.

*Grand Marnier is a brandy-based French liqueur flavored with orange peel. It pairs particularly well with chocolate. Other orange liqueurs or orange juice would work in this frosting, if desired.

Note: To make the orange curl garnish, use a citrus peeler to peel strips of rind from an orange; or peel 1 orange with a knife, leaving white pith on fruit. Cut orange rind into long, thin strips. Wrap rind strips tightly around a pencil to create curls. Freeze briefly; then remove orange rind strips from pencil.

Frozen White
Chocolate-Cherry
Terrine

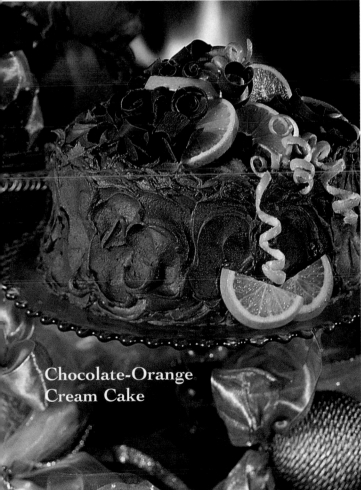

Chocolate-Orange
Cream Cake

Frozen White Chocolate-Cherry Terrine

This frozen molded dessert is chock-full of coconut candy bars, cherries, and white chocolate.

    1 tablespoon butter or margarine
    1 cup coarsely chopped pecans
    6 (1-ounce) squares white baking bar or
       white chocolate, chopped
 ⅓ cup milk
 ¾ cup chopped maraschino cherries
    2 (1.9-ounce) chocolate-coated coconut bars,
       frozen*
 2¼ cups whipping cream
 ⅓ cup sifted powdered sugar
       Hot fudge topping (optional)
       Garnish: 12 maraschino cherries with stems

Grease a 9" x 5" x 3" loafpan. Line pan with plastic wrap, making it smooth in pan and allowing it to extend slightly over edges of pan. Set aside.

Melt butter in a large skillet over medium heat; add pecans. Cook, stirring constantly, until pecans are toasted. Remove from heat; let cool completely.

Place chopped white chocolate in a small bowl. Bring milk to a simmer in a small heavy saucepan over medium-low heat. (Do not boil.) Remove from heat, and pour over chopped chocolate, stirring until chocolate melts. Let cool completely.

Press chopped cherries between paper towels to remove excess moisture. Chop frozen candy bars.

Beat whipping cream at high speed of an electric mixer until soft peaks form. Gradually add sugar, beating until blended. Gently fold in melted white chocolate mixture, chopped candy bars, and pecans; then fold in cherries.

Spoon mixture into prepared pan; cover and freeze 24 hours. To serve, dip pan in warm water 30 seconds. Invert loafpan onto a serving plate. Peel off plastic wrap. Cut terrine into ¾" slices. Drizzle fudge topping on each plate, if desired; top with a slice of frozen terrine. Garnish, if desired. **Yield:** 12 servings.

*For chocolate-coated coconut bars, we used Mounds.

Peanut Butter and Chocolate Truffle Torte

This is a dessert for the serious chocolate lover. One bite of this rich torte will remind you of a silky smooth truffle.

16 (1-ounce) squares semisweet chocolate, chopped
⅔ cup unsalted butter
½ cup creamy peanut butter
5 large eggs, lightly beaten
2 tablespoons all-purpose flour
   Peanut Butter Cream
   Garnish: toasted peanuts

Melt chocolate and butter in a large heavy saucepan over medium-low heat, stirring often. Remove from heat, and stir in peanut butter. Let cool slightly. Gradually add chocolate mixture to eggs, beating at medium speed of an electric mixer 10 minutes.

Fold flour into batter. Spoon batter into a greased and floured 9" springform pan.

Bake at 400° for 12 minutes for a gooey dessert, or 15 minutes for a firmer dessert. (Either way, torte will not be firm in center when removed from oven.) Let cool completely. Cover; chill thoroughly.

Remove sides of springform pan. Spoon warm Peanut Butter Cream onto each dessert plate. Top each with a slice of torte. Garnish, if desired. **Yield:** 10 servings.

Peanut Butter Cream
½ cup creamy peanut butter
1 cup sweetened condensed milk
¼ cup plus 2 tablespoons half-and-half

Melt peanut butter in a saucepan over medium-low heat, stirring constantly. Gradually stir in condensed milk and half-and-half; cook until heated. Remove from heat; serve warm. **Yield:** 1½ cups.

Peanut Butter and
Chocolate Truffle Torte

Half Dip Tips

Make some of the chocolate cookies in this chapter more irresistible with even more chocolate! Here are some ideas worth dipping into.

SPECKLED BISCOTTI (page 82):
•Melt 12 ounces chocolate candy coating or semi-sweet chocolate in top of a double boiler over hot water. Remove from heat. Fill a large mug with melted chocolate coating. Dip biscotti halfway into coating. Shake off excess coating, and let dry on wax paper over a wire rack. Refill mug as needed.

SPICY COCOA SNAPS (page 83):
•Follow procedure above, only using 10 ounces vanilla candy coating or white baking bars.

TIGER COOKIES (page 83):
•Place 1 cup milk chocolate morsels in a 2-cup glass measure. Microwave at HIGH 1 to 2 minutes or until melted, stirring every 30 seconds. Dip 20 cookies halfway into chocolate. Let dry on wax paper over wire racks. Repeat with another 1 cup morsels and remaining cookies. (It takes about 2 hours for milk chocolate coating to dry.)

DIPPED AND DRIZZLED COOKIES:
•Dip cookies as previously directed. Then seal ½ cup chocolate or vanilla morsels in a heavy-duty, zip-top plastic bag. Dip bag in very hot water 2 to 3 minutes or until chocolate melts. Remove bag from water; snip a tiny hole in one corner of bag. Drizzle chocolate over dipped cookies.

DIPPED AND DRIZZLED FRUIT:
•Dip various fruits such as fresh strawberries or dried apricots in melted semisweet chocolate. Let dry on wax paper-lined trays. Or drizzle fruit, if desired, as directed above.

Note: The amounts given above are enough for dipping one batch of each cookie recipe.

Satiny Mocha Torte

SWEETS IN SECONDS

A package of this. A jar of that.
How sweet it is to whip up these sensational
confections so quickly.

Ambrosia Pie

Satiny Mocha Torte

Convenience products do most of the work in this stunning four-layer cake with a shiny chocolate top.

- ¾ cup whole hazelnuts in the skins
- 1 (18.25-ounce) package devil's food cake mix without pudding*
- 2 (2.8-ounce) packages mocha mousse mix*
- 1⅓ cups milk
- ¾ cup whipping cream
- 1½ tablespoons Swiss-style flavored instant coffee powder*
- 6 (1-ounce) squares semisweet chocolate, chopped

Place hazelnuts in an ungreased 15" x 10" x 1" jelly-roll pan. Toast at 350° for 12 minutes or until skins begin to split. Transfer hot nuts to a colander; cover with a kitchen towel. Rub nuts briskly with towel to remove skins. Let nuts cool, and chop.

Grease and flour two 9" cakepans. Prepare cake mix according to package directions; pour into prepared pans. Bake at 350° for 30 minutes or until a wooden pick inserted in center comes out clean. Let cool in pans on wire racks 15 minutes; remove from pans, and let cool completely on wire racks.

Prepare mousse mix according to package directions, using 1⅓ cups milk; cover and chill.

Split cake layers in half horizontally to make 4 layers. Place 1 layer on a serving plate lined with wax paper. Spread one-third of mousse over layer. Repeat procedure with second and third layers and remaining mousse. Top stack with fourth layer. Chill 30 minutes.

Combine whipping cream and coffee powder in a saucepan; bring to a simmer over medium heat. Remove from heat; add chocolate. Let stand 1 minute. Stir until chocolate melts. Cool 30 minutes.

Pour chocolate glaze over torte, letting excess drip down sides onto wax paper. Using a small spatula, smooth excess glaze onto sides of torte. Gently press hazelnuts onto sides of glazed torte. Carefully pull wax paper from beneath torte. Store in refrigerator. **Yield:** one 9" torte.

*We used Duncan Hines devil's food cake mix, Nestle mocha mousse mixes, and General Foods International Coffees Suisse Mocha.

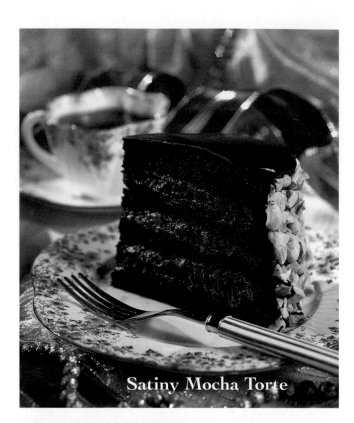

Satiny Mocha Torte

Gingerbread Fruitcake Cookies

Chewy Almond-
Fudge Bars

Gingerbread Fruitcake Cookies

This little drop cookie packs a big punch of ginger flavor.

1 (14-ounce) package gingerbread mix*
¼ cup plus 2 tablespoons water
¼ cup butter or margarine, melted
1 (4-ounce) container candied orange peel
½ cup golden raisins
½ cup chopped pecans
1½ cups sifted powdered sugar
2½ tablespoons lemon juice or orange juice

Combine first 3 ingredients, stirring until smooth. Fold in candied orange peel, raisins, and pecans.

Drop dough by rounded teaspoonfuls onto lightly greased cookie sheets.

Bake at 350° for 10 minutes. Let cool slightly on cookie sheets. Remove to wire racks, and let cool completely.

Combine powdered sugar and lemon juice, stirring until smooth. Drizzle over cooled cookies. **Yield:** 4 dozen.

*For gingerbread mix, we used Dromedary.

Chewy Almond-Fudge Bars

Coconut candy bars and toasted almonds give this brownie its personality. If you like firm bars, chill them.

1 (19.8-ounce) package chewy fudge brownie mix*
3 tablespoons vegetable oil
1 cup sweetened condensed milk
14 miniature dark chocolate coconut candy bars, chopped (1¼ cups)*
¾ cup chopped natural almonds, toasted

Prepare brownie mix according to package directions, reducing vegetable oil to 3 tablespoons; pour into a lightly greased 13" x 9" x 2" pan. Pour sweetened condensed milk over batter; sprinkle with chopped candy bars and almonds.

Bake at 350° for 36 to 38 minutes. Let cool completely in pan on a wire rack. Cut into bars. **Yield:** 2 dozen.

*For brownie mix, we used Duncan Hines. For miniature dark chocolate coconut candy bars, we used Mounds.

Chocolate-Peppermint Pudding Cake

This is one of those recipes you'll want to share with all your friends. It's easy to make and sinfully rich, and the peppermint imparts a taste of Christmas.

1 (18.25-ounce) package devil's food cake mix without pudding*
½ cup milk
3 tablespoons vegetable oil
⅓ cup crushed hard peppermint candies
⅓ cup sugar
2 tablespoons cocoa
1 cup boiling water
Vanilla ice cream
Garnish: additional crushed hard peppermint candies

Combine 2 cups cake mix, milk, and oil, stirring mixture well. (Reserve remaining 2 cups cake mix for another use.) Stir in ⅓ cup crushed peppermint candies. Spoon batter into a lightly greased 8" square pan.

Combine sugar and cocoa; sprinkle over batter. Pour boiling water over batter (do not stir).

Bake, uncovered, at 350° for 35 minutes. Let stand 5 minutes before serving. Serve warm pudding cake with vanilla ice cream. Garnish, if desired. **Yield:** 6 servings.

*For cake mix, we used Duncan Hines. There are 4 cups cake mix in the package. Seal the unused 2 cups mix in a zip-top plastic bag, and make the dessert again!

Chocolate-Peppermint Pudding Cake

Caramel-Apple Crumble

Caramel-Apple Crumble

Grab a spoon. Buttery apples await under melted caramels and a tender cake topping.

2   (28-ounce) jars fried apples
15   caramels, chopped*
½   cup cold butter or margarine, cut up
1   (18.25-ounce) package yellow cake mix without pudding*
½   cup chopped walnuts
    Vanilla ice cream (optional)
    Caramel sundae syrup (optional)
    Additional chopped walnuts

Spoon apples into a lightly greased 13" x 9" x 2" baking dish; sprinkle caramels over apples.

Chocolate-Cherry Bread Pudding

Cut butter into cake mix with a pastry blender until mixture is crumbly; stir in ½ cup walnuts. Sprinkle crumb topping over apple mixture.

Bake, uncovered, at 350° for 50 minutes to 1 hour or until crumb topping is golden.

Serve with vanilla ice cream and caramel syrup, if desired. Sprinkle each serving with additional walnuts. **Yield:** 12 servings.

*For caramels, we used Kraft. For cake mix, we used Duncan Hines.

Note: It's easy to snip caramels with kitchen shears.

Chocolate-Cherry Bread Pudding

This quick dessert received our highest rating, no doubt due to the juicy cherries and triple chocolate flavor.

1   (6-ounce) jar maraschino cherries
3   large eggs, lightly beaten
3   cups chocolate milk
¾   cup sugar
3   tablespoons butter or margarine, melted
1   tablespoon cocoa
6   cups cubed French bread
1   cup (6 ounces) semisweet chocolate morsels
    Garnishes: sweetened whipped cream, additional maraschino cherries

Drain cherries, reserving 1 tablespoon cherry juice. Coarsely chop cherries.

Combine eggs, 1 tablespoon cherry juice, milk, and next 3 ingredients in a large bowl, stirring well. Add bread cubes, and let stand 15 minutes, stirring occasionally. Stir in cherries and chocolate morsels.

Spoon mixture into a lightly greased 9" square pan. Bake, uncovered, at 350° for 50 minutes to 1 hour or until set. Serve bread pudding warm or at room temperature. Garnish, if desired. **Yield:** 9 servings.

Mint Chocolate Mousse Pie

This smooth and silky pie cuts best if you chill it overnight.

1   (11.1-ounce) package no-bake cheesecake
      mix*
⅓   cup butter or margarine, melted
2   tablespoons sugar
1   cup milk
½   cup chocolate mint-flavored syrup*
2   (1.55-ounce) minty milk chocolate bars
      with crunchy cookie bits, finely chopped*
      Garnishes: sweetened whipped cream,
      additional chopped chocolate bars

Combine graham cracker crumbs from cheesecake mix, butter, and sugar. Firmly press mixture in bottom and up sides of a 9" pieplate.

Combine milk and chocolate syrup in a medium bowl, stirring well. Add cheesecake filling mix; beat at low speed of an electric mixer until blended. Beat at medium speed 3 minutes. Fold in finely chopped chocolate. Spoon into prepared crust. Cover and chill at least 1 hour. Garnish, if desired. Before serving, dip bottom of pieplate in hot water for 30 seconds. **Yield:** one 9" pie.

*For cheesecake mix, we used Jell-O brand. For chocolate mint-flavored syrup and chocolate bars, we used Hershey's.

Peanut Butter Swirl Brownie Pie

Pockets of peanut butter dot this chocolaty pie, calling to mind a favorite candy.

½   (15-ounce) package refrigerated piecrusts
1   (15.5-ounce) package cheesecake swirl
      brownie mix*
¼   cup plus 1 tablespoon water, divided
¼   cup vegetable oil
2   large eggs
¼   cup plus 2 tablespoons crunchy peanut
      butter, divided
1   cup commercial hot fudge topping
      Vanilla ice cream

Fit piecrust into a 9" pieplate according to package directions. Fold edges under, and flute.

Combine brownie mix packet, 3 tablespoons water, oil, and 1 egg; stir until well blended. Set aside. Combine cream cheese filling mix packet, 2 tablespoons water, and 1 egg, stirring until smooth. Stir in ¼ cup peanut butter.

Spoon half of brownie mixture into piecrust; top with small mounds of cream cheese filling. Spoon remaining brownie mixture over filling. Cut through mixture in pan with a knife to create swirls.

Bake at 350° for 35 minutes. Cool on a wire rack.

Combine hot fudge topping and remaining 2 tablespoons peanut butter in a saucepan. Cook over low heat, stirring until smooth. Serve pie with ice cream and hot fudge sauce. **Yield:** one 9" pie.

*For brownie mix, we used Pillsbury.

Ambrosia Pie

Holiday fruit is blended with cream cheese and coconut, and frozen for dessert.

  1 (11-ounce) can mandarin oranges in light syrup
  1 (8¼-ounce) can crushed pineapple in heavy syrup
  1 (8-ounce) package cream cheese, softened
  1 (14-ounce) can sweetened condensed milk
2½ cups frozen whipped topping, thawed and divided
  ¾ cup flaked coconut, toasted
  1 (9-ounce) graham cracker crust (extra serving size)
     Garnishes: maraschino cherries, pecan halves, additional toasted flaked coconut

Drain oranges and pineapple, reserving 2 table-spoons pineapple syrup. Gently press oranges and pineapple between paper towels to remove excess moisture.

Beat cream cheese at medium-high speed of an electric mixer until creamy. Gradually add reserved pineapple syrup and milk, beating until smooth. Fold in 1½ cups whipped topping. Gently fold in orange-pineapple mixture and ¾ cup coconut. Spoon filling into crust. Cover; freeze until firm.

Let pie stand at room temperature 20 minutes before serving. Dollop remaining 1 cup whipped topping on top of pie. Garnish, if desired. **Yield:** one 9" pie.

Carrot Cake Roulage

Carrot cake claims a new shape in this jellyroll. Look for the lavish cream cheese frosting rolled up inside.

    Vegetable cooking spray
4 large eggs
½ cup water
1 (18.25-ounce) package spice cake mix*
1 cup grated carrot
3 tablespoons powdered sugar, divided
1 (15¼-ounce) can crushed pineapple in heavy syrup
2 (16-ounce) cans cream cheese frosting
½ cup chopped pecans, toasted
    Powdered sugar
    Garnish: toasted chopped pecans

Coat two 15" x 10" x 1" jellyroll pans with cooking spray; line with wax paper, and coat wax paper with cooking spray. Set aside.

Beat eggs in a large bowl at medium-high speed of an electric mixer 5 minutes. Add water, beating at low speed until blended. Gradually add cake mix, beating at low speed until moistened. Beat mixture at medium-high speed 2 minutes. Fold in grated carrot.

Spread batter evenly in prepared pans (layers will be thin). Bake, one at a time or in separate ovens, at 350° on the middle rack 13 minutes or until each cake springs back when lightly touched in center.

Sift 1½ tablespoons powdered sugar in a 15" x 10" rectangle on a cloth towel; repeat with 1½ tablespoons sugar and a second towel. When cakes are done, immediately loosen from sides of pan, and turn each out onto a sugared towel. Peel off wax paper. Starting at narrow end, tightly roll up each cake and towel together; place, seam side down, on wire racks to cool completely.

Drain pineapple, reserving ¼ cup syrup. Press pineapple between paper towels to remove excess moisture. Combine pineapple, cream cheese frosting, and ½ cup pecans; stir well.

Unroll cakes; brush each lightly with 2 tablespoons reserved pineapple syrup. Spread each cake with half of frosting mixture. Reroll cakes without towels; place, seam side down, on serving plates.

Cover and chill at least 1 hour. Dust cakes with additional powdered sugar before serving. Garnish, if desired. **Yield:** 2 cake rolls.

*For spice cake mix, we used Duncan Hines.

Note: This recipe makes 2 cake rolls, so it's ideal for a make-ahead dessert for a crowd. Or give the second roll as a gift.

Carrot Cake Roulage

White Chocolate
Charlotte Russe
with Cranberry
Sauce

White Chocolate Charlotte Russe With Cranberry Sauce

It seems fitting to tie such a delicate molded dessert with sheer ribbon for a beautiful presentation.

    2 (3.4-ounce) packages fat-free white
       chocolate instant pudding mix*
  2¾ cups milk
    2 teaspoons grated orange rind
    2 tablespoons Grand Marnier or other orange
       liqueur or orange juice, divided
    1 teaspoon vanilla extract
    1 cup whipping cream, whipped
   19 ladyfingers, split
    1 (12-ounce) tub cranberry-orange crushed
       fruit*

Prepare both packages of pudding mix according to package directions, using 2¾ cups whole milk instead of skim milk. Stir in orange rind, 1 tablespoon Grand Marnier, and vanilla. Gently fold in whipped cream.

Line bottom and sides of a 9" springform pan with ladyfingers (see note at right). Spoon pudding mixture into pan. Cover and chill at least 4 hours or until dessert is set.

Combine crushed fruit and remaining 1 tablespoon Grand Marnier, stirring well. Place dessert on a serving platter; carefully remove sides of pan. Serve with cranberry sauce. **Yield:** 12 servings.

*We used Jell-O brand pudding mixes and Ocean Spray crushed fruit in a plastic tub. Find the crushed fruit on the aisle with canned fruit.

Note: Here's an easy way to arrange ladyfingers in the springform pan. Simply remove rows of connected ladyfingers intact from their package, and unfold them into bottom of pan, and then again around sides of pan.

What's Charlotte Russe? It's a Russian molded dessert that begins with a ladyfinger shell and is filled with a whipped cream or a custard-gelatin filling. When ready to serve, cut dessert into wedges, or just use a large spoon.

Brandied
Eggnog
Trifle

Brandied Eggnog Trifle

Serve this plush pudding in wine glasses.

1 quart refrigerated eggnog, divided
2 envelopes unflavored gelatin
¼ cup brandy, divided
1 teaspoon vanilla extract
3 cups frozen whipped topping, thawed and divided
1 (16-ounce) frozen pound cake loaf, thawed
5 cups sliced fresh strawberries
1 cup strawberry preserves
   Garnish: toasted sliced almonds

Place 1 cup eggnog in a medium saucepan; sprinkle with gelatin. Let stand 1 minute. Cook over low heat, stirring gently, until gelatin completely dissolves. Stir in remaining eggnog, 2 tablespoons brandy, and vanilla. Remove from heat. Chill until consistency of unbeaten egg white (about 15 minutes). Fold in 1 cup whipped topping; chill until mixture is softly set. Cut pound cake into cubes; set aside.

To layer dessert in a trifle bowl, arrange enough strawberry slices, cut sides out, to go around lower edge of a 4-quart trifle bowl. Place half of pound cake cubes in bowl; sprinkle with 1 tablespoon brandy.

Combine remaining strawberries and preserves. Spoon half of strawberry mixture over pound cake; top with half of eggnog mixture. Top with remaining pound cake, and sprinkle with remaining 1 tablespoon brandy. Spoon remaining strawberry mixture over pound cake; then spoon remaining eggnog mixture over strawberries.

Spread remaining 2 cups whipped topping over trifle. Cover and chill at least 1 hour. Garnish, if desired. **Yield:** 14 servings.

Variation: To serve this trifle in wine glasses, layer ingredients as directed for trifle bowl, dividing them evenly to fill the glasses. Or prepare dessert in trifle bowl as directed, and just spoon mixture into wine glasses (this method won't be quite as neat).

Note: Two 16-ounce packages of frozen whole strawberries can be substituted for 5 cups fresh strawberries. Just place whole strawberries in bottom of bowl. (If you slice them, they become mushy.)

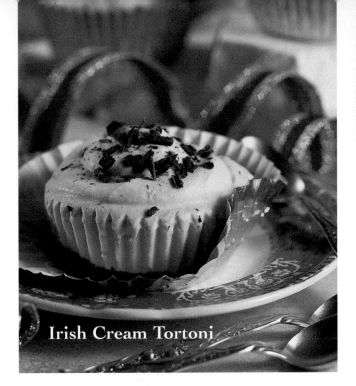

Irish Cream Tortoni

Date-Nut Kahlúa Turnovers

Irish Cream Tortoni

*These frozen dessert cups, which hail from Italy, take on
the addition of a smooth liqueur and a cookie base.*

  ¾ **cup crushed cream-filled chocolate sandwich
     cookies (10 cookies)**
  ¼ **cup boiling water**
  1 **teaspoon instant coffee granules**
  3 **tablespoons grated semisweet chocolate,
     divided**
  ¼ **cup Irish cream liqueur**
  1½ **cups whipping cream**
  ¼ **cup sifted powdered sugar**

Line 12 (3") muffin cups with foil muffin liners.
Sprinkle 1 tablespoon cookie crumbs in bottom of
each liner; press lightly.

  Combine boiling water and coffee granules, stirring until coffee granules dissolve. Add 1 tablespoon
grated chocolate, stirring well. Stir in liqueur, and let
cool completely.

  Beat whipping cream at high speed of an electric
mixer until foamy; add sugar, beating until soft peaks
form. Gently fold in liqueur mixture. Spoon evenly
into muffin liners. Cover; freeze until firm.

  Remove from freezer, and let stand 5 minutes
before serving. Sprinkle evenly with remaining 2
tablespoons grated chocolate. **Yield:** 12 servings.

Date-Nut Kahlúa Turnovers

*Kahlúa, the king of coffee liqueurs, gives a glisten to this
date-nut filling that's tucked in flaky triangles.*

  ⅓ **cup dark corn syrup**
  2 **teaspoons butter or margarine, melted**
  1½ **teaspoons Kahlúa or other coffee-flavored
     liqueur or strong brewed coffee
     Dash of salt**
  1 **large egg, lightly beaten**
  1 **(8-ounce) package chopped dates (1⅓ cups)**
  ½ **cup chopped pecans**
  1 **teaspoon water**
  1 **(17¼-ounce) package frozen puff pastry,
     thawed**
  1 **tablespoon sugar**

Combine first 4 ingredients; stir well. Add half of
beaten egg; stir well. Stir in dates and pecans. Combine
remaining half of egg with 1 teaspoon water; set aside.

  Roll each sheet of pastry into a 12" square on a
lightly floured surface. Cut each square into 9 (4")
squares. Spoon 1 heaping tablespoon date mixture into
center of each square; brush edges of pastry with egg
mixture. Fold each square of pastry into a triangle;
seal edges with a fork. Brush top of each pastry with
remaining egg mixture, and sprinkle with sugar. Place
pastries on an ungreased baking sheet.

  Bake at 400° for 10 to 12 minutes or until puffed
and golden. **Yield:** 18 turnovers.

THE
JOY OF
GIVING

Christmas in Fredericksburg: A Sprig of Herbal Heaven

To inspire you to make your own gifts, we traveled to the Fredericksburg Herb Farm in the Texas Hill Country.

FREDERICKSBURG HERB FARM OWNERS Bill and Sylvia Varney want to encourage each of us to let herbs and flowers enhance our lifestyle. For Bill and Sylvia, herbal creations are particularly appropriate Christmas gifts. "These humble plants touch life's ho-humness and elevate it to the heavenly, bringing a simple yet profound joy to our existence," says Bill.

The Varneys experience—and spread—that joy at their herb farm located on 14 pastoral acres in the rolling hills just outside Austin. Bill and Sylvia have transformed a historical 1880s limestone farmhouse into an old-fashioned apothecary and tearoom, as well as a culinary store, which sells award-winning vinegars, mustards, and oils. They've added a candle shop and bookstore and opened the Herb Haus, a quaint bed-and-breakfast—and oh, what delightful herb-inspired treats await guests!

Visitors at the Herb Farm are invited to sip fresh herb lemonade and enjoy soothing piano music while they stroll through the spacious gardens, savor the aroma of the rosemary bushes, and enjoy a fresh-from-the-garden luncheon. Afterwards, perhaps they'll indulge in a luxurious herb-infused facial or aromatherapy massage at the Quiet Haus.

And whether they're at the bed-and-breakfast or the store, guests always fall under the spell of the crisp, citrusy fragrance of the Varneys' signature pot-pourri. It's an Herb Farm best-seller; take one whiff from a homemade batch and you'll know why.

Note: For essential oils and dried herbs, see Sources on page 154.

Herb Garden Potpourri

The Varneys' potpourri recipe is based on the liberal use of natural essential oils. A variety of herbs and whole rose petals adds beautiful color and texture to the fragrant blend.

   1 ounce powdered orris root
   6 drops rosemary essential oil
   6 drops lemon essential oil
   6 drops lavender essential oil
   6 drops orange essential oil
2½ cups dried lemon verbena
1½ cups dried lemon balm
   1 cup dried rosemary
   1 cup dried lavender
   ½ cup dried thyme
   ½ cup dried sage
     Dried rose petals
     Dried yarrow blossoms
     Dried bay leaves
   ¼ cup cinnamon powder
   ½ cup lovage root
   6 tablespoons grated orange peel

To make potpourri, combine orris root and oils in small bowl; set aside. Combine lemon verbena, lemon balm, rosemary, lavender, thyme, and sage in large bowl. Add handful of rose petals and yarrow blossoms. Sprinkle in bay leaves. Add cinnamon, lovage, and orange peel. Stir orris root mixture into large bowl; cover bowl. Let stand out of direct light for 5 days, stirring occasionally.

Package in decorative baskets or cellophane bags tied with ribbon.

In 1985, newlyweds **Bill and Sylvia Varney** opened a store on Main Street in historic Fredericksburg, Texas, selling old-world toiletries, natural seasonings, vinegars, and small pots of herbs. Growing at a Jack-and-the-Beanstalk pace, their business moved to the Herb Farm in 1991, the same year their Edible Flower Herb Vinegar won the Outstanding Condiment Award from the National Association for the Specialty Food Trade.

"Our farm is about renewal," says Bill. "Using herbs in our gift recipes awakens all the senses."

"We offer quick ideas for people who 'don't cook,' but who enjoy delicious meals," says Sylvia. Here, the Varneys share recipes for an aromatic spiced tea, a pair of herbal butters, and herbed walnuts.

Fruit and Spice Herb Tea

- 2 cups dried lemon verbena leaves
- 1 cup dried chamomile
- 1 cup dried orange zest
- 3 tablespoons whole cloves, crushed
- 1 (6") cinnamon stick, crushed

To blend the tea, combine all ingredients in a bowl; mix well. Package in a tightly covered decorative tin, and include a card with the following directions: Shake the tin well to mix ingredients. Spoon 1 teaspoon of tea mix per 1 cup of boiling water into cup. Pour boiling water over tea mix; stir gently. Steep for 5 to 10 minutes. **Yield:** 4 cups tea mix.

Petal Honey Butter

- 1 cup firmly packed rose petals
- ⅓ cup unsalted butter, softened
- ½ cup honey

To make the butter, remove the white "nails" from the rose petals. Combine petals, butter, and honey in food processor. Process until well blended. Chill thoroughly. Package in an airtight container. **Yield:** 1¼ to 1½ cups.

Sweet Herb Butter

- ½ cup unsalted butter, softened
- 2 tablespoons minced fresh lemon balm or lemon verbena
- 1 tablespoon strawberry jam or marmalade
  Grated zest of 1 lemon
- 1 tablespoon brandy (optional)
- 2 tablespoons toasted almonds or pecans

To make the butter, combine all ingredients in a bowl; mix well. Chill thoroughly. Package in an airtight container. **Yield:** ¾ to 1 cup.

Rosemary Walnuts

- ¼ cup cold unsalted butter, cut into 4 pieces
- 2 tablespoons very finely minced fresh rosemary
- ¼ teaspoon salt
- ⅛ teaspoon ground red pepper
- 2 cups walnut halves

To make the butter, combine first 4 ingredients in foil-lined jellyroll pan. Bake at 400° until butter melts; remove from oven. Add walnuts; toss to coat. Bake 6 to 9 minutes or until walnuts are lightly toasted, stirring at 3-minute intervals. Let cool. Package in an airtight container. **Yield:** 2 cups.

Fruit and Spice Herb Tea

Rosemary Walnuts

Sweet Herb Butter

Petal Honey
Butter

"We use the farm's 'cream of the crop' in our vinegars," Bill says. "From growing to harvesting to producing, we do everything right here." Garnishes are Texas-sized and fresh picked. You can duplicate these results in your own kitchen with the Varneys' recipes.

HERBAL VINEGARS

Basic Directions:

To make herbal vinegars, fill a clean, sterilized glass bottle or jar with fresh herbs. Use ⅔ white vinegar to ⅓ white or red wine to make vinegar more mellow. Pour vinegar/wine mixture over herbs; bruise herbs with a wooden spoon.

Cover container and store in a cool, dark place at room temperature. Stir mixture once every 4 or 5 days with a wooden spoon. The vinegar will be ready in 3 to 6 weeks, depending upon how strong you want it to be.

Filter/strain herbs from vinegar. (A coffee filter and funnel work well.)

Place a few clean, fresh herb sprigs in a clean, attractive bottle. Pour vinegar over sprigs.

Basic Herb Vinegar

- ½ cup fresh sweet basil
- ½ cup fresh rosemary
- ¼ cup fresh Mexican mint marigold (tarragon)
- 4 bay leaves
- ¼ cup fresh oregano
- 1 teaspoon mixed peppercorns
- 1 teaspoon whole cloves

To make vinegar, follow Basic Directions.

"We encourage visitors to literally stop and smell the roses . . . and for the adventurous, to bathe in them, too!" says Bill.

Olé Herb Vinegar

1½ cups assorted peppers
1 cup fresh cilantro
2 cloves garlic
1 to 2 green onions
3 to 4 sprigs thyme

To make vinegar, follow Basic Directions.

Festive Herb and Edible Flowers Vinegar

1 cup chives
½ cup fresh dill
1 cup fresh mint
½ cup fennel seeds

To make vinegar, follow Basic Directions. When bottling, add fresh, clean blossoms from chives, dill, borage, lavender, and mint.

Vinegar for the Bath

"In the bath, vinegar is a natural way to calm, soften, and deodorize the skin, to soothe and deep cleanse pores . . . and refresh the spirit," says Sylvia.

2 ounces fresh rosemary
2 ounces fresh mint
2 ounces rose geranium
2 ounces rose petals
2 ounces lavender
6 cups apple cider vinegar or white vinegar
1 cup rose water

To make bath vinegar, mix herbs and flowers together; add vinegar. Bottle and steep in refrigerator for 3 to 6 weeks. Strain and rebottle. Add a few fresh herb sprigs and rose water.

Winter Blooms in Painted Pots

Amaryllis and paperwhite bulbs are delightful presents, thanks to their glorious display and delicious freshness. Plant the bulbs in pots you've painted for a lively gift that will fit everyone.

John Floyd, editor of *Southern Living* and an experienced horticulturist, knows exactly how to ensure that flowering bulbs get the right start and enjoy proper growing conditions. He shares his knowledge here. Attach a photocopy of John's tips to your gift plant with a pretty ribbon.

Note: During late November and December, you can purchase plants already in bloom (like the poinsettia and cyclamen pictured on these pages) at most garden centers. But it's more thoughtful to give bulbs whose buds are ready to open so their recipient can enjoy the full show.

AMARYLLIS

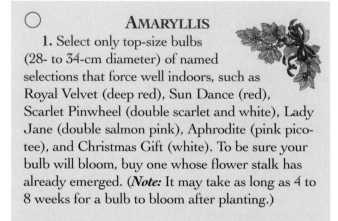

1. Select only top-size bulbs (28- to 34-cm diameter) of named selections that force well indoors, such as Royal Velvet (deep red), Sun Dance (red), Scarlet Pinwheel (double scarlet and white), Lady Jane (double salmon pink), Aphrodite (pink picotee), and Christmas Gift (white). To be sure your bulb will bloom, buy one whose flower stalk has already emerged. (*Note:* It may take as long as 4 to 8 weeks for a bulb to bloom after planting.)

2. Plant the bulb in a pot filled with potting soil to within 1" of the rim. Make sure the top half of the bulb sits above the soil line and that the pot has a drainage hole. Water the bulb once, and then place the pot in a warm room where temperature ranges from 70° to 75°. When the flower stalk appears, move the pot to a bright window. Now, temperature needs to be between 60° and 65°.

3. Keep the soil moist. Start feeding monthly with water-soluble 20-20-20 fertilizer after the plant begins to bloom. Cut the stalks after the flowers fade, but don't disturb the leaves.

4. After the last spring frost, take the pot outside to a sunny spot. Water and feed throughout spring and summer. In September, stop feeding and watering. When the leaves yellow, cut them off and take the pot inside to a dry, dark place. After about a month, move it to a warm room, water once, and wait. As soon as the bulb sprouts, carry it to a bright window and wait for another season of bloom.

PAPERWHITES

Fill the pot (with drainage hole) ¾
full with potting soil. Set the bulbs on
top of the potting soil, shoulder to shoulder.
Pour gravel up to the necks of the bulbs to
hold them in place.

Water well, and repeat when the soil feels dry.
Move the pot to a bright window as soon as
leaves and buds begin to appear.

PAINTED POTS

Hand-paint terra-cotta pots with a variety of
designs to make ideal gift containers for your
plants. The pots pictured here will give you
some ideas.

To paint terra-cotta pots, use your choice of
acrylic paints. Stripes and circles are easy to paint
freehand. After the paint has dried, spray pots
with clear acrylic.

Skin Soothers He'll Love

PAMPER THE MEN ON YOUR CHRISTMAS list with soothing products that are easy to make and guaranteed to please. With these recipes developed by **Janice Cox,** author of two books and a monthly magazine column on beauty and skin care, you have the secret to luxurious products at a fraction of the retail cost. The handy tote is made from laminated fabric, so it's water-resistant.

Shaving Cream

You will need:
¼ cup stearic acid powder (available at craft stores in the candlemaking section)
1 to 2 teaspoons light oil (optional)
1 cup boiling water
1 teaspoon borax (available in detergent section of grocery stores)
2 tablespoons grated bar soap
1 to 2 drops essential oil (optional)
container with tight-fitting lid

1. To mix, in double boiler, melt stearic acid powder until it dissolves into a clear liquid. Set aside. For a moisturizing shaving cream, add light oil to stearic acid powder before melting.

Combine boiling water, borax, and soap, stirring until borax and soap are completely dissolved.

Pour soap solution into blender and blend at low speed for approximately 1 minute. Mixture will become white and frothy. With blender on, slowly pour stearic acid liquid into soap mixture. To make scented shaving cream, add essential oil to mixture in blender. Blend at high speed until smooth and creamy. Pour into clean bowl and stir well. Let cool completely. Mixture will become thicker as it cools.

When cool, spoon cream into clean jar with tight-fitting lid.

2. To use, wet face with warm water and smooth shaving cream over face. (**Note:** If cream is not used every day, it may need to be stirred before using.) **Yield:** 8 ounces.

Pumice Stone Hand Scrub

You will need:
small pumice stone (We used one 5" x 1" x ½".)
1 cup grated bar soap
½ cup borax (available in detergent section of
    grocery stores)
container with lid

1. To mix, place pumice stone in sturdy plastic
bag and secure opening. With hammer on a hard
surface, smash stone to a fine powder. You should
have approximately ¼ cup of "pumice powder."

Combine pumice powder, soap, and borax. Mix
well. Pour into clean, dry container.

2. To use, pour small amount of mixture into
hand, and mix with warm water to form lather;
then rinse hands thoroughly with water. **Yield:**
12 ounces.

Woodland Aftershave

You will need:
1 cup vodka (For sensitive skin, substitute witch
    hazel for vodka.)
½ tablespoon dried rosemary
1 teaspoon vanilla extract
1 tablespoon dried pine needles
container with tight-fitting lid

Note: For dried herbs, see Sources on page 154.

1. To mix, combine all ingredients and pour into
clean jar with tight-fitting lid. Place container in cool,
dark place for 2 weeks.

After 2 weeks, pour liquid through paper coffee
filter-lined strainer to remove all solid ingredients.
Pour liquid into clean bottle with tight-fitting lid.

2. To use, splash on face after shaving. **Yield:**
8 ounces.

Tote Bag

You will need:
pattern and diagrams on page 147
⅝ yard 45"-wide laminated fabric
1 (78") leather boot lace

Note: All seams are ½". For fabric, see Sources on
page 154.

1. To cut out tote, using pattern, from fabric, cut
2 (9") circles and 2 (13⅝" x 20") rectangles.

To mark casing opening, at sides of each rectangle,
cut notches in seam allowance 7¼" from bottom edge
and 8" from bottom edge.

To aid in attaching bottom circles to sides, mark
quarters on circles. (To mark quarters: fold circle in
half; clip ends. Refold circle so notches match; clip
ends. See Diagram 1.)

2. To sew sides, with right sides facing and raw
edges aligned, sew rectangles together along 1 (20")
side, leaving open between notches for casing. Sew
opposite side, leaving open between notches for
casing, and, near top of rectangle, leaving 4" section
open for turning (see Diagram 2). Press seams open.

Make notches on tube to align with quarter notches
on circles. (Notch at side seams, then fold tube so
that side seams match; notch ends.)

3. To sew bottom to tote, with right sides facing,
sew 1 circle inside 1 end of tube, matching notches.
Repeat to sew second circle to other end of tube; turn
tote right side out.

4. To make casing, slip 1 half of tube into other
half, aligning circles to form bottom of tote. (The
4" opening will be on inside of tote.) Slipstitch opening closed. Press fold at top edge of tote. (Casing
opening should be 2" from top.) Topstitch 2" from
fold. Topstitch again 2¾" from fold to form casing.

5. To thread ties, cut leather lace in 2 equal pieces.
Run 1 piece through casing all around tote so that
both ends emerge from same opening. Run second
leather piece so that its ends emerge from opposite
opening. Pull each piece of leather to close bag.

Tile Treasure Boxes

Colorful tiles make terrific boxes for all sorts
of keepsakes. Glue tiles together, add a handle on top,
and you've got a gift that is quick to make
and a treat to receive.

You will need:
clear silicone glue
6 (4"-square) tiles for large box
6 (3"-square) tiles for small box
masking tape
variety of small tiles to decorate sides and lids
marbles or decorative drawer pulls

Note: You can purchase tiles from most home improvement stores.

1. To make box, glue 1 tile to each side of 1 bottom tile, forming box. Let dry. To reinforce corners, apply glue along inside corners. Let dry. (*Note:* Use heavy food cans to hold tiles in place as you glue them together. Use masking tape to temporarily secure decorative tiles while glue dries.) Referring to photo, glue additional tiles of different shapes and sizes on box sides and lid, as desired. Let dry.

2. To make handle, glue marbles or decorative drawer pull in place in center of tile lid. Let dry. If desired, glue marbles or round drawer pulls on bottom for feet. Let dry.

Wiry Wreaths to Wear

Once you've got the twist of this design, it's simple to make a holiday pin or pendant.

To make the circle a pin, attach a pin back. Use a thin satin cord for the pendant. You'll find most of the supplies (washers and wire!) for this gift at the local hardware store.

You will need:
16- and 20-gauge brass wire
wire cutter
needle-nose pliers
½" brass flat washer (for pin)
1" hardened steel flat washer (for pendant)
clear household cement
satin-finish clear polyurethane spray
¾" pin back (for pin)
1 yard satin cord (for pendant)

1. **To make wire shapes,** from both gauges of wire, cut several 3" lengths. To bend wire lengths into S shapes, hold 1 end of wire with pliers and bend to form a large spiral, leaving 1" unbent at opposite end. Hold unbent wire end with pliers and bend to form a small spiral in opposite direction of large spiral.

Bend some wire lengths to form coil shapes to fill in spaces between spiral shapes on wreath. To form coils, bend wire as for spirals, cutting away excess wire when desired coil size is achieved.

2. **To determine placement on washer,** place larger gauge spirals at 3 points around washer/wreath. Fill in with smaller gauge spirals and coils. Cut and bend additional pieces, if needed.

3. **To attach shapes to washer,** remove wire shapes from washer, keeping their placement in mind. Following manufacturer's directions, apply thin layer of glue to surface of washer. Replace wire pieces on washer in positions determined in Step 2, making adjustments for fit as necessary. Let dry overnight.

4. **To finish,** following manufacturer's directions, spray wreath with 1 coat of clear polyurethane. Let dry. For pin, glue pin back to back of wire wreath. Let dry. For pendant, thread cord through center of wreath or through coils at top of wreath, and knot ends together.

Peppermint Stress-Relief Collar

Heated in the microwave, this tension-reducing collar—with its pleasing peppermint fragrance—will provide a measure of heavenly peace.

You will need:
pattern on page 149
graph paper
½ yard velvet
disappearing-ink fabric marker
1¼ yards lace
1 pound pearl tapioca (Pearl tapioca is available in grocery and health food stores. "Minute" tapioca is not suitable for this project.)
peppermint essential oil (optional)
funnel

Note: All seam allowances are ½". For velvet and essential oil, see Sources on page 154.

1. **To cut collar pieces,** using graph paper, enlarge pattern. Using pattern, cut 2 collar pieces from fabric. Using fabric marker, transfer topstitching lines from pattern to 1 collar piece.

2. **To attach lace to collar,** pin edge of lace to ½" seam line of 1 collar section along center front and outer edges only, as indicated by solid lines on pattern. Position edge of lace ½" from center front edges of collar. Adjust lace so motifs will match at front. Baste lace to collar on seam line. With right sides facing and raw edges aligned, stitch collar pieces together, leaving 3" opening at center back for turning. Trim seams and clip curves. Turn collar

and press lightly, using scrap piece of velvet on ironing board to prevent crushing velvet. Topstitch along transferred topstitching lines (see pattern).

3. **To fill collar with tapioca pearls,** sprinkle tapioca pearls with a few drops of peppermint oil, if desired. (Essential oil is highly concentrated, so a few drops will do.) Using funnel and working over bowl, fill collar with tapioca pearls, evenly distributing tapioca into channels. Slipstitch collar opening closed.

4. **To use,** heat collar in microwave on high heat for approximately 1 minute. Do not overheat. Collar will stay warm for 15 to 20 minutes.

Herbal Bathtub Tea

Steep one of these tea bags in a hot bath to release the soothing scent of lavender. A dressed-up terra-cotta saucer makes a clever tray for gift-giving.

To make each bathtub tea bag, from **white muslin,** cut 2 (4" x 4") squares, using pinking shears. Topstitch squares together at bottom and sides ⅝" from outside edge, leaving top open for filling. Fill stitched bag with **dried lavender.** Cut a 7" length of **narrow gold cording.** Center 1 end of the cording in the top of the bag between the layers of muslin. Topstitch ⅝" from the outside edge, catching the cording in the seam. Tie a knot in the end that remains free. To finish, glue a **decorative tassel** at the center top of the tea bag. (*Note:* We used tassels cut from a row of fringed trim.)

To make the container, dab **gold paint or Rub 'n Buff** on a **terra-cotta plant saucer** to cover. Let dry. Glue **decorative trim** around the rim of the saucer. Place a plush washcloth in the saucer, and stack bathtub tea bags on top for an attractive gift presentation.

Scentsational Gifts

Wax crystals are the speedy secret behind the Teacup Candle; cinnamon and cloves are the fragrant filling for Scented Coasters.

Teacup Candle

You will need (for each):
12 ounces wax crystals (Candle Magic® used)
¼ ounce essential oil of your choice
teacup and saucer
precoated wick (Candle Magic® used)

1. To make candle, pour 12 ounces of wax crystals into a zip-top plastic bag with ¼ ounce of essential oil. Close bag and shake, mixing wax crystals and oil. Pour wax crystals into teacup, filling to within ½" of brim. Smooth surface of wax crystals. Push wick into center of wax crystals until end of wick meets teacup bottom. Trim top of wick to within ½" of wax crystals.

2. To seal surface of candle, hold hot iron on medium setting 4" above wax crystals for approximately 3 minutes. Heat from iron will melt top layer of wax crystals, preventing crystals from spilling out.

Scented Coasters

You will need (for 6 coasters):
⅓ yard fabric (Allow extra yardage for centering design motifs.)
polyester batting
6 tablespoons whole cloves
3 cinnamon sticks, broken into small pieces
ribbon (optional)

Note: For fabric, see Sources on page 154.

1. To make coasters, from fabric, cut 12 (5") squares. From batting, cut 6 (5") squares. For each coaster, layer 2 fabric squares (right sides together) and top with batting square. Using ¼" seam allowance, stitch along all sides, leaving 2" opening for turning. Trim batting close to stitching. Trim corners, turn, and press. Repeat for remaining coasters.

2. To add spices, combine cloves and cinnamon stick pieces. Spoon approximately 1 tablespoon of spice mixture into each coaster at opening. Slipstitch opening closed. Tie stack of coasters together with ribbon, if desired.

Woodland Log Tote

Sturdy canvas makes a reliable firewood carrier that stitches up in less than an hour.

You will need:
pattern on page 152
1 yard canvas
**¼ yard each green, red, and
   blue check flannel**
¼ yard fusible web
size 100 sewing machine needle
2¾ yards 1"-wide belt webbing

1. To cut out tote, from canvas, cut 2 (16" x 34") rectangles. Using pattern, cut 1 tree from each color of check flannel. Using pattern, from fusible web, cut 3 trees.

2. To position trees, arrange trees in desired pattern at center top of 1 canvas piece, leaving 4" clearance on both sides and 1¾" at top. Following manufacturer's directions, fuse trees to canvas. Using size 100 sewing machine needle and widest zigzag stitch, machine-stitch around each tree, reducing stitch width at angled points and indentations.

3. To sew tote, using ½" seam allowance, with right sides facing and raw edges aligned, machine-stitch canvas rectangles together, leaving 4" opening for turning. Trim corners, grade seam allowances, turn, and press. Topstitch ¼" and then ½" along all sides.

4. To make handles, beginning on back side of tote, stitch webbing to canvas 2¼" from outside edges, leaving approximately 16" of webbing at each end for handles. Where webbing ends meet, turn top piece under ¼" and overlap ends. Stitch in place. Reinforce handles by stitching over previous topstitching.

Stamped-and-Ready Christmas Card

This new "inking-off" stamping technique produces a holiday card with a hand-painted look.

You will need (for each card):
2 sheets colored paper (2 different colors)
1 sheet matte-finish card-weight paper
deckle-edge scissors (optional)
glue
rubber stamps: at least 1 with bold solid design and 1 with more detailed design
multicolor stamp pad

Note: For stamps and stamp pad, see Sources on page 154.

1. To make card, fold 1 sheet of colored paper in half widthwise to form card. Then cut 2 rectangles— 1 from second sheet of colored paper and 1, smaller than the first, from card-weight paper. Use deckle-edge scissors to cut rectangles, if desired. Glue colored paper rectangle to card front.

2. To create design, with chosen stamps in mind, plan your design. Move bold design stamp in up-and-down motion across multicolor stamp pad. Firmly press detailed stamp directly to inked bold design stamp. (This technique removes the color from the first stamp, leaving the impression of the second stamp.)

3. To imprint design on paper, using stamp with bold "double-stamped" design, firmly press motif to card-weight paper rectangle. Any number of stamps may be used to create your "picture." Let ink dry. Center stamped rectangle on top of card and glue in place.

Sprightly Stationery

Tissue-wrapped envelopes add a refined note to this card gift
set that gets its sparkle from embossing stamps and powder.

You will need:
bold design rubber stamp
embossing stamp pad
blank note cards
embossing powder
embossing tool
decorative tissue paper
freezer paper
envelope to fit note card
blank stickers
glue stick

Note: For stamps and embossing powder, see Sources
on page 154.

1. To make each card, press rubber stamp onto
embossing pad. Imprint image onto card in desired
design. Shake embossing powder over stamped design,
pouring excess powder back into bottle. Following
manufacturer's directions, heat stamped and embossed
areas with embossing tool.

2. To make each envelope, crush tissue paper until
very wrinkled. Smooth tissue paper flat with hands.
Place tissue paper on top of freezer paper and press,
using a medium-hot iron. Do not use steam. (The
freezer paper will melt to the tissue.)

Carefully undo envelope. Lay envelope flat and
trace onto paper to create a template. Place template
on tissue/freezer paper and trace pattern. Cut out
pattern and, following folds of original envelope, fold
tissue/freezer paper to create customized envelope.
Place blank stickers on front of envelope for address.
Use a glue stick to seal flap.

Fancy Wraps for Festive Treats

FOOD IS ALWAYS AN APPROPRIATE GIFT. After all, everyone loves to eat. But gift food needn't be homemade to be heartfelt. During the holidays, your schedule may not include much time in the kitchen. Here are six smart ways to package purchased foods that will ensure your reputation as a thoughtful (and creative) giver.

Lanterns light the way for innovative food containers. After the goodies are gone, the "wrappings" become attractive decorative items for the house. These are filled with red and green hard candies.

You can also use these clever containers to hold cheese straws, nuts, or cookies. But don't stop there! You can create one-of-a-kind containers using **coffee or tea cups, terra-cotta pots, or small bowls** wrapped in cellophane and tied with bright ribbon.

Picture holiday treats, such as Heavenly Chocolate Chunk Cookies (page 84) or brightly colored Christmas candies, framed in handsome **photo boxes.** Later, the boxes are the place for sweet visual memories of the season. (***Note:*** Empty Christmas card boxes, lined with crisp tissue paper, make beautiful gift containers as well.)

Fill a **gallon-size zip-top plastic bag** with Speckled Biscotti (page 82) or tasty purchased cookies. Place the filled bag between **2 square napkins** and tie the corners with **decorative ribbons.** Attach an **ornament** at 1 corner, if desired.

A **wire basket** filled with Sugar Crinkles (page 72) will bring good cheer to all who are lucky enough to receive it. Wrap cookies in plastic wrap, and lace colorful ribbons through the wire for a quick gift that overflows with charm. If you don't have a wire basket, try weaving ribbon through the slats of a **straw market basket** for a similar look.

Note: For lanterns, photo boxes, and fruit ornaments, see Sources on page 154.

The customary bottle of wine takes on distinctive style when tucked in a **twig basket spray-painted gold.** (*Note:* A good time to buy baskets at great prices is just after Easter. Spray-paint baskets gold or silver for Christmas.) Wire **faux grape clusters** (found at most discount and import stores) to the handle, and tie on a sparkling ribbon for a spirited presentation. A package of cocktail crackers along with the wine is an appropriate addition.

Flea markets, tag sales, and antique shops offer a wide selection of quaint **glass jars.** Fill jars with spiced apples, homemade jam, or fruit candies, and top them with **ornaments** that hint at the treats within.

Fruit-and-Foliage Package Toppers

Adding inexpensive permanent fruits to wrappings conveys that the gift inside is meant for a special person.

To add fruit embellishments to your presents, cut the desired fruit from the main stem of a **fruit pick,** leaving about a 1½" stem on it. Tie the stem into the knot of the bow. For **fruit clusters,** tape the stems of several different fruits together, and tie them into the bow. To attach other fruits, such as **apples and pears,** simply glue each piece to the package as desired. To add **beads,** attach them to a string or a stem, tape them together to form a cluster, and tie them into the bow. For the most secure arrangement, knot the ribbon over the stems, and tie a bow over the knot.

Note: You can find fruit picks, permanent fruits, and beads at discount and import stores.

SHIPPING YOUR GIFTS

Now that you've wrapped your gift to perfection, make sure it stays that way in the mail. Follow these steps to ensure that it arrives at its destination in pristine condition:

◄ Place the wrapped package in a sturdy cardboard box. Be sure that the box is deep enough so the bow won't be crushed when the top is closed.

◄ Stuff crumpled kraft paper or newspaper around the package to keep it from shifting in transit.

◄ Carefully tape the cardboard top closed. Don't use string or ribbons on the outside of the cardboard box. And be sure to write "To" and "From" information on the inside of the box as well as the outside.

CHRISTMAS DINNER

Menu

Serves 8

Pear, Hazelnut, and Blue
Cheese Salad

Orange-Glazed Roasted Turkey

Pan Gravy

Classic Cornbread Dressing

Sweet Potatoes Laced with Grand Marnier

Roasted Brussels Sprouts with Garlic and
Slivered Almonds

Commercial Crescent Rolls

Apple-Berry Cobbler with Vanilla Bean Hard Sauce

White Chocolate Pecan Pie

Wine   Water   Coffee

The vivid colors and flavors of this feast will warm your soul.

This year's menu features a turkey that gains a golden skin from roasting in a honey-orange glaze. And it promises to yield moist, succulent slices, thanks to its cheesecloth covering. (See step-by-step photos on page 137.) Brussels sprouts and sweet potatoes splash bright color onto the plate. And the dessert choices are positively Southern—a fruity cobbler (below) and a pie perched with pecans and bits of buttery white chocolate.

Dinner Plans

THREE DAYS BEFORE CHRISTMAS:
• Place turkey in refrigerator to thaw, if preparing a frozen bird.

TWO DAYS BEFORE CHRISTMAS:
• Prepare Vanilla Bean Hard Sauce; cover and chill.
• Bake Cornbread for Classic Cornbread Dressing.

THE DAY BEFORE CHRISTMAS:
• Prepare and bake White Chocolate Pecan Pie.
• Prepare Raspberry Vinaigrette for salad; cover and chill.
• Toast hazelnuts for salad; remove skins, and chop.
• Prepare Sweet Potatoes Laced with Grand Marnier, but don't bake, following make-ahead directions. Cover and chill.

CHRISTMAS MORNING:
• Wash brussels sprouts, and remove any wilted outer leaves. Trim and cut a shallow X in bottoms of sprouts; cover and chill.
• Prepare Pear, Hazelnut, and Blue Cheese Salad; cover and chill.

FOUR HOURS BEFORE THE MEAL:
• Prepare turkey, and place in oven to roast.
• Finish preparing cornbread dressing. Chill. Bake dressing during the last hour the turkey roasts.
• Prepare Apple-Berry Cobbler, but don't bake. Set aside.

ONE HOUR BEFORE THE MEAL:
• Remove sweet potato mixture from refrigerator, if following make-ahead directions. Add topping.

THIRTY MINUTES BEFORE THE MEAL:
• Transfer roasted turkey to serving platter to "rest." Prepare Pan Gravy.
• Bake sweet potatoes.
• Roast Brussels Sprouts with Garlic and Slivered Almonds.

FIFTEEN MINUTES BEFORE THE MEAL:
• Bake crescent rolls; place in basket to keep warm.
• Reheat cornbread dressing briefly, if necessary.
• Remove hard sauce from refrigerator to soften slightly.

DURING THE MEAL:
• Bake Apple-Berry Cobbler.

Pear, Hazelnut, and Blue Cheese Salad

To keep pears looking fresh once you've sliced them, dip slices in lemon water (¼ cup water plus 1 tablespoon lemon juice).

 1 cup whole hazelnuts in the skins
 8 cups mixed salad greens (such as red leaf, green leaf, Bibb)
 2 ripe red Bartlett pears, unpeeled and thinly sliced
 2 ripe green pears such as Anjou, unpeeled and thinly sliced
 1 (4-ounce) package blue cheese, crumbled
    Raspberry Vinaigrette
    Freshly ground pepper (optional)

Place hazelnuts in an ungreased 15" x 10" x 1" jellyroll pan. Bake at 350° for 12 to 15 minutes or until skins begin to split. Transfer hot nuts to a colander, and cover with a kitchen towel. Rub nuts briskly with towel to remove skins; chop nuts.

Combine salad greens, sliced pears, hazelnuts, and blue cheese in a large bowl; toss gently. Pour Raspberry Vinaigrette over salad just before serving; toss gently. Sprinkle with freshly ground pepper, if desired. **Yield:** 8 servings.

Raspberry Vinaigrette
 ½ cup vegetable oil
 ¼ cup raspberry vinegar
 2 tablespoons honey
 ¼ teaspoon pepper
 ⅛ teaspoon salt

Combine all ingredients in a jar; cover tightly, and shake vigorously. Cover and chill thoroughly. **Yield:** ¾ cup.

Orange-Glazed Roasted Turkey

The cheesecloth covering on this turkey acts as a blanket that locks in juices. The roasted results are incredibly moist.

      Cheesecloth
 1½ cups orange juice
  1 (12-pound) turkey
     Salt and pepper
  3 tablespoons vegetable oil
 1½ cups chicken or turkey broth
  ½ cup butter or margarine, melted
  ¼ cup orange marmalade
  3 tablespoons honey
  2 teaspoons grated orange rind
  1 tablespoon coarse-grained mustard
     Garnishes: flowering kale, baby artichokes, red grapes
     Pan Gravy

Cut a 36" length of cheesecloth; unfold to a single layer (measuring 36" square). Fold cheesecloth in half crosswise; fold in half lengthwise to make an 18" square. Pour orange juice into a small bowl; submerge cheesecloth square in orange juice, and let soak 5 minutes.

Remove giblets and neck from turkey; reserve for making homemade broth, if desired. Rinse turkey thoroughly with cold water; pat dry. Sprinkle cavity with salt and pepper. Place turkey, breast side up, in a greased broiler pan. Tie legs together with heavy string, or tuck them under flap of skin; wrap a small piece of aluminum foil around ends of legs. Lift wingtips up and over back, and tuck under bird. Brush turkey with oil; add broth to pan.

Lift cheesecloth out of orange juice, and squeeze lightly, leaving it very damp; reserve orange juice in bowl. Add butter and next 4 ingredients to orange juice; stir well. Brush turkey lightly with orange glaze mixture. Unfold cheesecloth to 18" square. Spread cheesecloth over most of turkey, covering legs and wings. Brush cheesecloth and exposed parts of turkey with orange glaze mixture; pour remaining glaze over covered breast of turkey.

Insert a meat thermometer into meaty portion of thigh, making sure it does not touch bone. Bake at 325° on bottom oven rack until thermometer registers 170° (2½ to 3 hours), basting cheesecloth and exposed areas of turkey every 30 minutes with pan juices. (Cheesecloth will become very brown as turkey roasts.)

Carefully remove and discard cheesecloth. Cut string holding legs together; remove small piece of aluminum foil. Baste turkey heavily with pan drippings. Bake turkey at 325° for 30 additional minutes or until thermometer registers 180°, basting heavily with pan drippings every 10 minutes. (Turkey skin can overbrown easily, so watch carefully.)

When turkey is done, let stand in pan 15 minutes; then carefully transfer to a serving platter. Brush again with pan drippings; reserve remaining pan drippings for Pan Gravy. Cover turkey with foil while preparing gravy. Garnish platter with kale, baby artichokes, and red grapes, if desired. Serve turkey with Pan Gravy. **Yield:** 10 servings.

Note: If you have a larger or smaller turkey, adjust roasting time accordingly, and remove cheesecloth for the last 30 minutes of roasting. The turkey browns quickly after removing cheesecloth, so baste often at that point.

Pan Gravy
After the turkey is roasted and "resting" on a serving platter, reuse the broiler pan to make this golden gravy.

 3 **tablespoons all-purpose flour**
 ⅓ **cup water**
    Pan drippings
 2 **cups chicken or turkey broth**
 1 **teaspoon browning-and-seasoning sauce**
 ½ **teaspoon salt**
 ½ **teaspoon pepper**

Combine flour and water in a small bowl, stirring well; set aside.

Pour pan drippings into a large measuring cup; skim off fat. Add enough water to pan drippings to equal 3 cups. Combine pan drippings, chicken broth, and remaining 3 ingredients in broiler pan; stir in flour mixture.

Using two burners, bring gravy to a boil over medium-high heat, stirring constantly to loosen any browned particles in pan. Reduce heat, and boil 5 minutes or until thickened. **Yield:** 3½ cups.

Note: If you use only one burner to make gravy, it may take longer for it to thicken.

PREPARING THE TURKEY

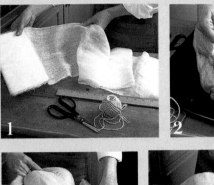

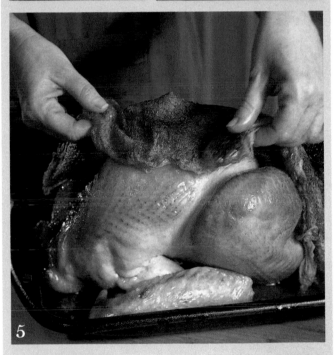

1. Cut a 36" length of cheesecloth. Find cheesecloth at hardware stores or grocery stores; or see Sources on page 154.
2. Tie legs together with heavy string.
3. Lift wingtips up and over back, and tuck under bird.
4. Spread soaked cheesecloth square over most of turkey, covering legs and wings.
5. Cheesecloth will be very brown when you remove it from turkey.

Classic Cornbread Dressing

If you're short on time, use packaged cornbread mix (to yield about 5 cups coarsely crumbled cornbread) instead of making homemade Cornbread below.

- 1   cup diced celery
- 1   cup diced onion
- ½ cup butter or margarine, melted
- 5   large kale leaves or spinach leaves, chopped
  Cornbread
- 7   slices white bread, toasted and coarsely crumbled or cut into ½" cubes (4 cups)
- ½ cup chopped walnuts, toasted
- ½ cup chopped fresh parsley
- 3   tablespoons chopped fresh sage
- ¾ teaspoon salt
- ½ teaspoon pepper
- 2   large eggs, lightly beaten
- 2   to 3 cups chicken broth

Cook celery and onion in butter in a large skillet over medium heat until tender, stirring occasionally. Add kale, and cook, stirring constantly, 3 minutes or until kale wilts. Remove from heat.

Coarsely crumble Cornbread into a large bowl. Add kale mixture; stir well. Add toasted breadcrumbs and next 6 ingredients. Stir in enough broth to moisten dry ingredients as desired. (For moist dressing, add the entire 3 cups broth.)

Spoon dressing into a greased 13" x 9" x 2" pan. Bake, uncovered, at 325° for 1 hour or until top begins to brown. **Yield:** 10 servings.

Cornbread
- 2   cups yellow cornmeal
- ¾ cup all-purpose flour
- 1½ tablespoons sugar
- 1   tablespoon baking powder
- ½ teaspoon salt
- ¼ teaspoon baking soda
- 1   large egg, lightly beaten
- 2   cups buttermilk
- 2   tablespoons butter or margarine, melted
  Shortening

Combine first 6 ingredients in a large bowl. Combine egg, buttermilk, and butter; add to dry ingredients, stirring just until moistened.

Heavily grease a 10" cast-iron skillet with shortening. Place in a 425° oven 5 minutes or until very hot (almost smoking). Remove skillet from oven, and spoon batter into hot skillet. Bake at 425° for 25 minutes or until lightly browned. Let cool in pan. Cover loosely, and let stand overnight. **Yield:** 10 servings or 5 cups coarsely crumbled cornbread.

Sweet Potatoes Laced with Grand Marnier

Orange liqueur, nutmeg, and pecans naturally dress up sweet potatoes.

- 6   medium-size sweet potatoes (3 pounds)
- 3   tablespoons butter or margarine, melted
- ¾ cup sugar
- 3   tablespoons Grand Marnier (orange liqueur) or orange juice
- 1   teaspoon grated orange rind
- ¼ teaspoon salt
- ¼ teaspoon ground nutmeg
- 1   large egg, lightly beaten
- ½ (14-ounce) can sweetened condensed milk
- 1   cup firmly packed brown sugar
- 1   cup chopped pecans
- ⅓ cup all-purpose flour
- ⅓ cup butter or margarine, melted
- ¼ teaspoon ground nutmeg

Cook potatoes in boiling water to cover in a Dutch oven 30 to 40 minutes or until tender; drain. Let cool slightly. Peel potatoes, and place in a large bowl. Add 3 tablespoons butter, and mash. Add ¾ cup sugar and next 6 ingredients; mash again, or beat at medium speed of an electric mixer until smooth. Spoon mixture into a lightly greased 2-quart casserole.

Combine brown sugar and remaining 4 ingredients; sprinkle over sweet potato mixture. Bake, uncovered, at 425° for 30 minutes or until thoroughly heated, shielding with aluminum foil after 20 minutes to prevent excessive browning. **Yield:** 8 servings.

Make-Ahead Directions: Prepare sweet potato mixture, and spoon into greased casserole. Cover and chill overnight. Remove from refrigerator 30 minutes before baking; add brown sugar topping. Bake casserole as directed above.

Roasted Brussels Sprouts with Garlic and Slivered Almonds

Roasting slightly chars and subtly sweetens these sprouts.

2½ pounds fresh brussels sprouts (about 6
    cups) or 4 (8-ounce) packages frozen
    brussels sprouts, thawed
⅓ cup olive oil
⅓ cup slivered almonds
4 large cloves garlic, minced
3 tablespoons butter or margarine, melted
¼ teaspoon salt
¼ teaspoon pepper

If using fresh brussels sprouts, wash them thoroughly; remove discolored leaves. Cut off stem ends, and slash bottom of each sprout with a shallow X. Toss brussels sprouts with oil in a shallow roasting pan, coating well.

Bake at 425° for 15 minutes. Transfer to a serving bowl; cover and keep warm.

Meanwhile, brown almonds and garlic in butter in a small skillet over medium heat; add salt and pepper. Pour garlic mixture over brussels sprouts; toss gently. Serve immediately. **Yield:** 8 servings.

Make-Ahead Directions: Prepare recipe several hours before meal. Just before serving, place in a microwave-safe dish; cover with heavy-duty plastic wrap. Microwave at HIGH 3 to 4 minutes or until thoroughly heated, stirring after 2 minutes.

139

Apple-Berry Cobbler with
Vanilla Bean Hard Sauce

Apple-Berry Cobbler with Vanilla Bean Hard Sauce

Butter and sugar crown this cobbler as a hard sauce bold with black flecks of vanilla bean.

- 1 cup all-purpose flour
- ½ cup wheat germ
- 1 teaspoon baking powder
- ¼ teaspoon salt
- ½ cup butter or margarine, softened
- ½ cup sugar
- 1½ tablespoons milk
- 1 large egg
- 1¾ pounds cooking apples, peeled, cored, and sliced (6 cups)
- 2 cups fresh or frozen cranberries, partially thawed
- 1 cup firmly packed brown sugar
- 1 teaspoon vanilla extract
- ½ teaspoon ground cinnamon
- 2 teaspoons cornstarch
- ¼ cup water
- Vanilla Bean Hard Sauce (optional)

Combine first 4 ingredients; set aside.

Beat butter at medium speed of an electric mixer until creamy. Gradually add sugar; beat well. Add milk and egg; beat well. Stir in flour mixture; set batter aside.

Combine sliced apple and next 4 ingredients in a large bowl. Combine cornstarch and water. Add to apple mixture; stir well. Spoon apple mixture into a lightly greased 11" x 7" x 1½" baking dish. Drop batter by spoonfuls over fruit mixture. Bake, uncovered, at 350° for 45 or 50 minutes or until golden. If desired, serve warm with Vanilla Bean Hard Sauce or ice cream. **Yield:** 8 servings.

Vanilla Bean Hard Sauce

- 1 whole vanilla bean, split lengthwise
- 2 cups sifted powdered sugar
- 1 cup butter or margarine, softened

Scrape tiny vanilla bean seeds into sugar; stir well. Combine vanilla sugar and butter in a mixing bowl. Beat at medium speed of an electric mixer until blended. Transfer to a serving dish. **Yield:** 1⅔ cups.

White Chocolate Pecan Pie

Chunks of white chocolate in the filling glamorize this Southern pie.

- ½ (15-ounce) package refrigerated piecrusts
- ¼ cup butter or margarine, melted
- ½ cup sugar
- ½ cup light corn syrup
- ¾ cup chopped pecans, toasted
- 1 teaspoon vanilla extract
- ¼ teaspoon salt
- 2 large eggs, lightly beaten
- 6 (1-ounce) premium white chocolate baking squares, chopped*
- 1 cup pecan halves

Unfold piecrust, and press out fold lines; sprinkle with flour, spreading over surface. Place crust, floured side down, in a 9" pieplate; fold edges under, and flute. Bake at 450° for 5 minutes.

Combine butter, sugar, and corn syrup; cook over low heat, stirring constantly, until sugar dissolves. Let cool slightly. Add chopped pecans and next 3 ingredients; stir well. Pour filling into prebaked piecrust; sprinkle with two-thirds of chopped white chocolate. Top with pecan halves.

Bake at 325° for 50 to 55 minutes or until set. Cover with aluminum foil during last 10 minutes of baking to prevent excessive browning. Let cool on a wire rack.

Place remaining chopped white chocolate in a small heavy-duty, zip-top plastic bag; seal bag. Submerge bag in hot water until chocolate melts. Remove bag from water. Snip a tiny hole in one corner of bag, using scissors; drizzle chocolate over pie. **Yield:** one 9" pie.

*For white chocolate, we used Baker's.

Note: One 6" vanilla bean equals about 1 tablespoon extract, if you want to substitute extract in the cobbler's hard sauce at left.

The greens of the season set this holiday table with nature's richness.

Fashion this verdant centerpiece of fruits and vegetables (at right), and your guests will be green with envy. Stack two cake pedestals; top with a Styrofoam cone. Using wooden skewers or floral picks, build a tower of green by attaching the following items to the cone: bundles of asparagus and green beans, brussels sprouts, baby artichokes, broccoflower, peppers, pears, cut limes and kiwifruit, sprigs of greenery, and Granny Smith apples. Accent the centerpiece with paperwhites, holly berries, star fruit slices, and ribbon.

For place card holders, set aside eight food items from the centerpiece such as pears, baby artichokes, or small bundles of beans. Use strands of plastic gold beads to tie the fruits or vegetables, along with hole-punched place cards, onto napkins.

Patterns

Framed in Gold

Instructions begin
on page 68.

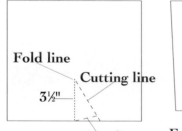 

Fold line

Cutting line

3½"

Trim line

Fold stand out to use.

Star Billing

Instructions begin
on page 26.

Patterns are full-size.

Striped Glass Cake Dome

Instructions begin
on page 40.

Painted Holly Place Settings

Instructions begin
on page 41.

Pattern is full-size.

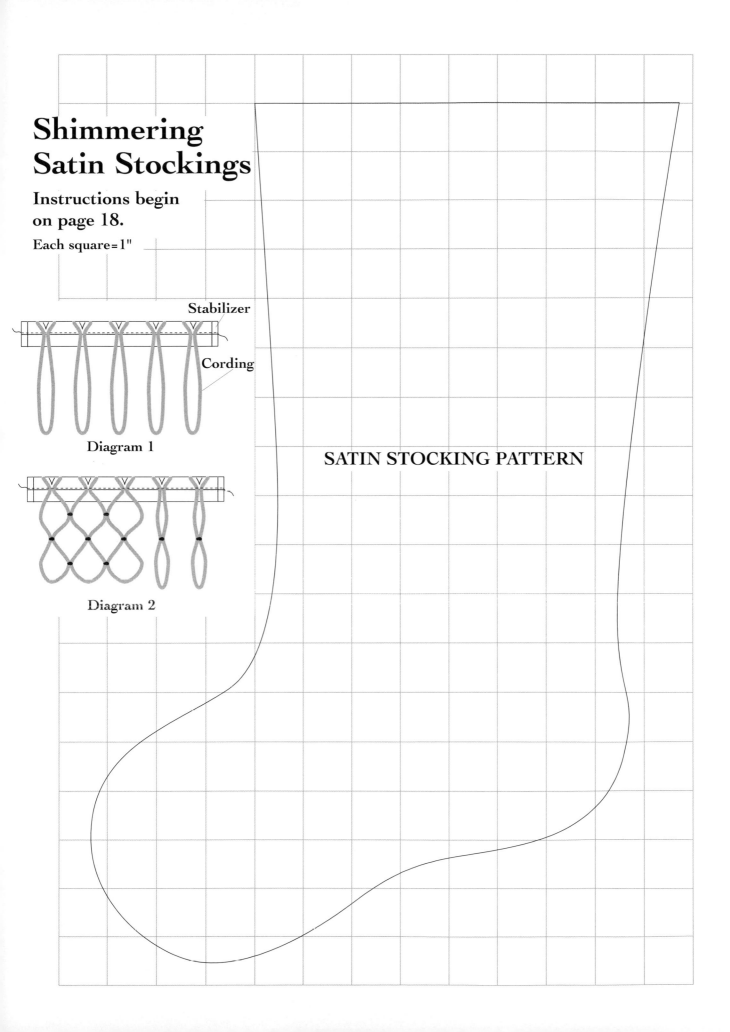

Shimmering Satin Stockings

Instructions begin
on page 18.

Each square=1"

Stabilizer

Cording

Diagram 1

Diagram 2

SATIN STOCKING PATTERN

Felt Filigree Tree Skirt

Instructions begin on page 65.

Each square = 1"

Pattern diagram

TREE SKIRT PATTERN
(¼ of pattern)

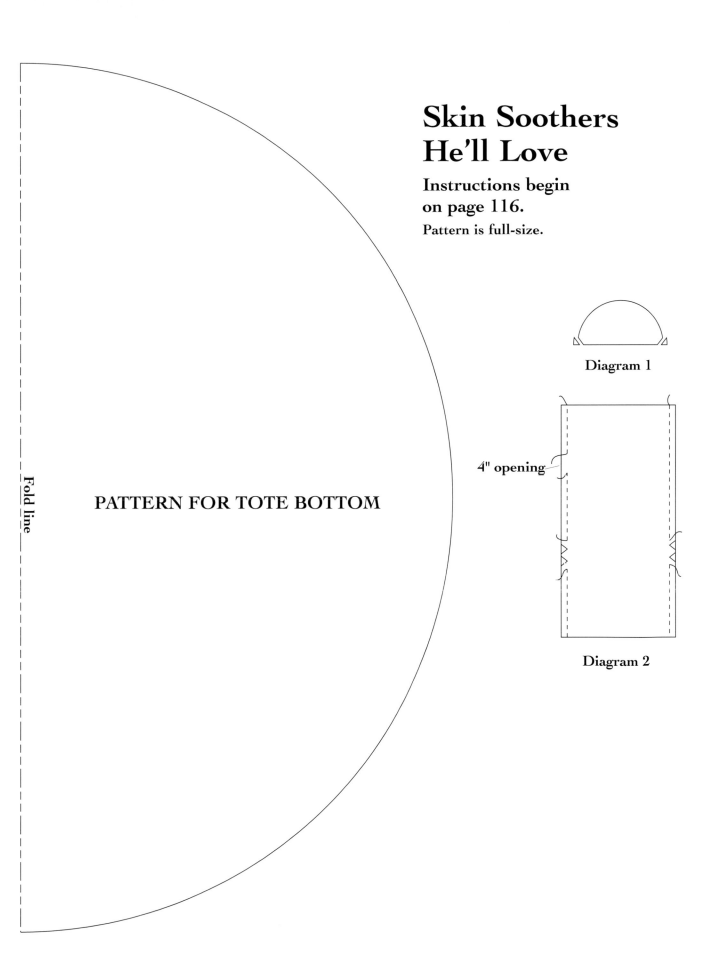

Skin Soothers
He'll Love

**Instructions begin
on page 116.**

Pattern is full-size.

Diagram 1

Fold line

PATTERN FOR TOTE BOTTOM

4" opening

Diagram 2

Christmas Memories Album

Instructions begin on page 62.

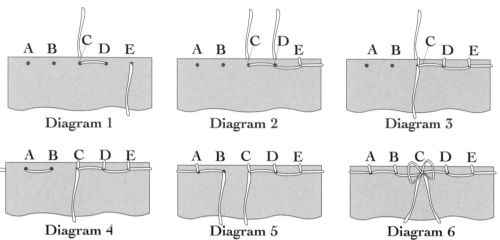

A B C D E Diagram 1

A B C D E Diagram 2

A B C D E Diagram 3

A B C D E Diagram 4

A B C D E Diagram 5

A B C D E Diagram 6

1. Fold ribbon in half lengthwise. From front of album, lace 1 half of ribbon through hole C up to halfway mark and back up through hole D and back down through hole E; pull ribbon taut.

2. Wrap ribbon around spine of album at E, and lace back down through E. Wrap ribbon around top edges of album, and lace back down through E. Lace up through D; pull ribbon taut.

3. Wrap ribbon around spine of album at D, and lace back down through D. Lace up through C.

Wrap ribbon around spine of album at C and lace up again through C.

4. With the other half of ribbon, lace up through hole B and back down hole A; pull ribbon taut.

5. Wrap ribbon around spine of album at A, and lace back down through A. Wrap ribbon around

edges of album, and lace ribbon back down A and up through B; pull ribbon taut.

6. Wrap ribbon around spine of album at B, and lace back up through B. Feed end of ribbon through a finished lace at hole C, and tie ribbon ends into a knot. Finish by tying ribbon into bow.

Ribbon-Trimmed Table Linens

Instructions begin on page 38.

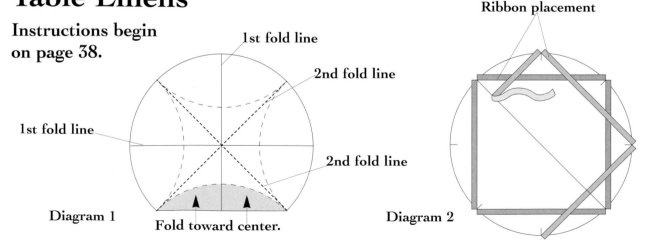

1st fold line

2nd fold line

1st fold line

2nd fold line

Fold toward center.

Diagram 1

Ribbon placement

Diagram 2

String-of-Lights Cookie Wreath

Recipe is on page 48.

Pattern is full-size.

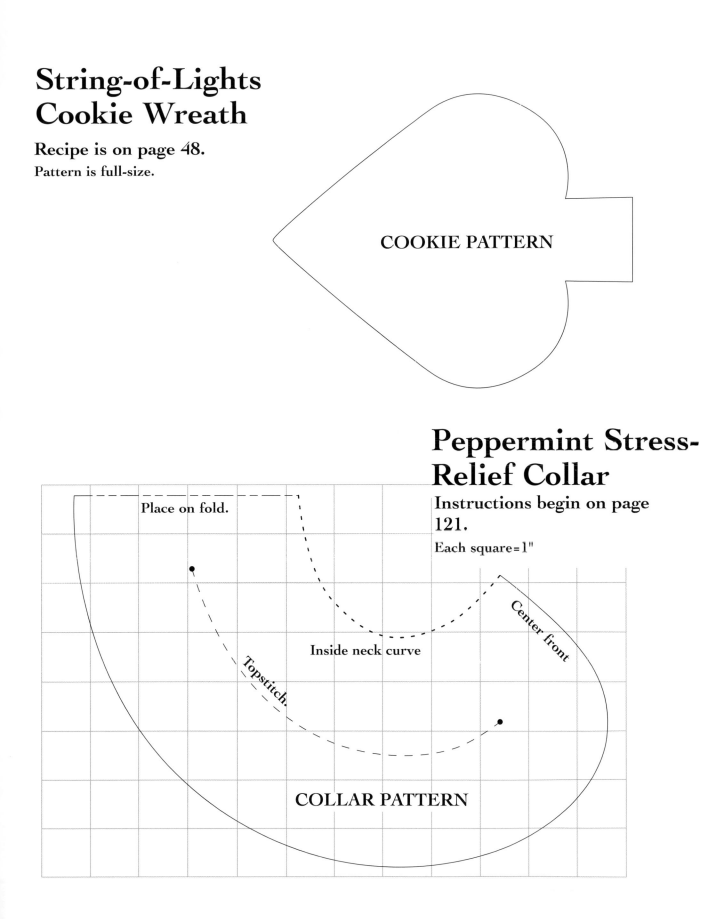

COOKIE PATTERN

Peppermint Stress-Relief Collar

Instructions begin on page 121.

Each square=1"

Place on fold.

Inside neck curve

Center front

Topstitch.

COLLAR PATTERN

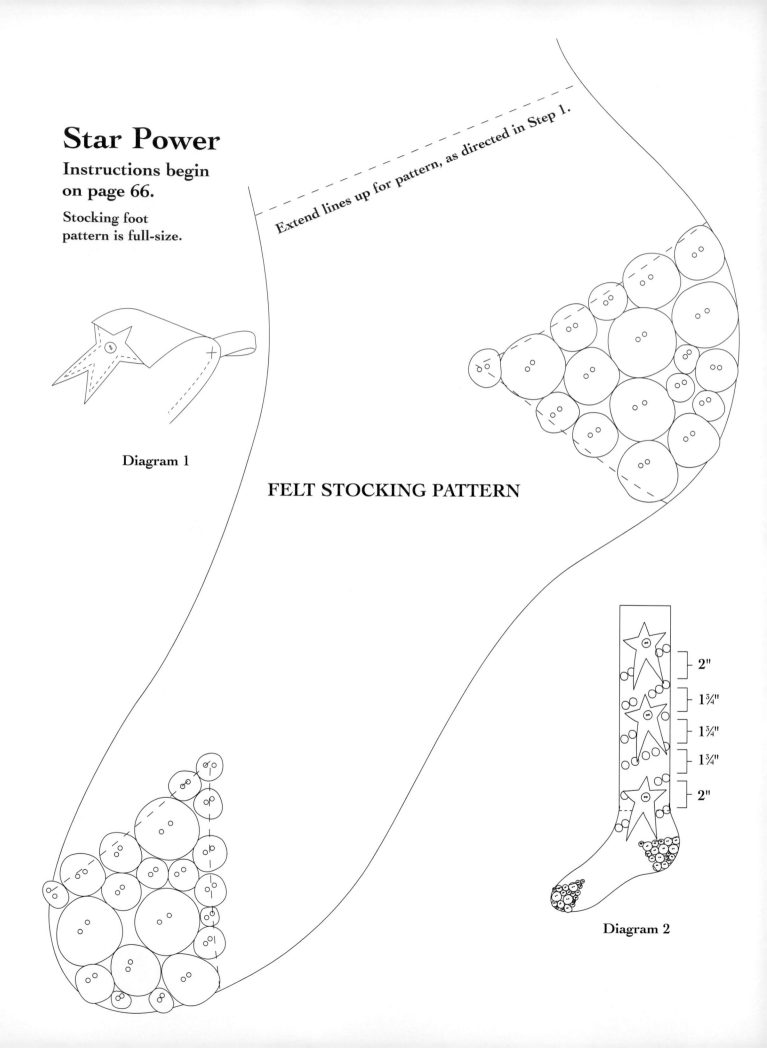

Star Power

**Instructions begin
on page 66.**

**Stocking foot
pattern is full-size.**

Diagram 1

Extend lines up for pattern, as directed in Step 1.

FELT STOCKING PATTERN

2"

1¾"

1¾"

1¾"

2"

Diagram 2

Star Power

Instructions begin on page 66.

Pattern is full-size.

FELT STAR PATTERN

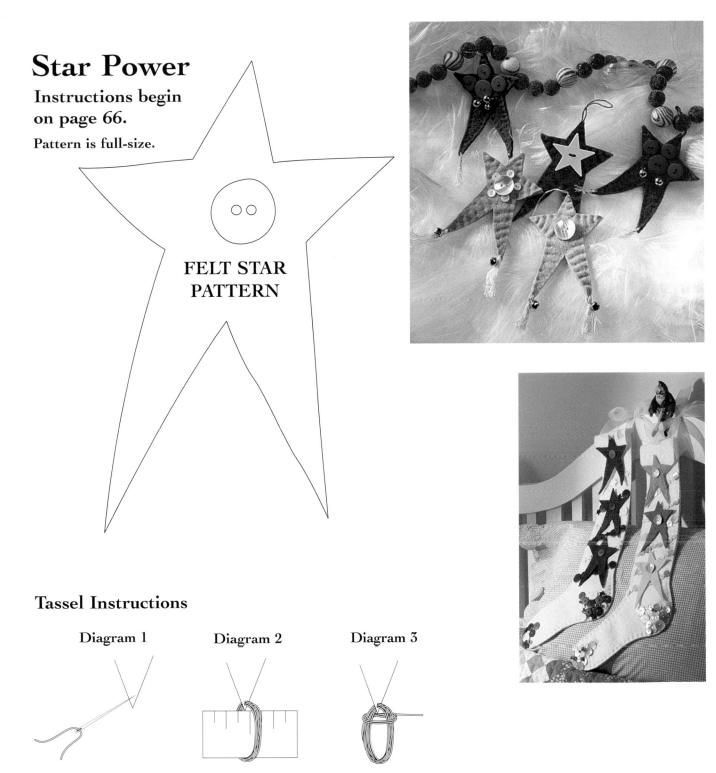

Tassel Instructions

Diagram 1

Diagram 2

Diagram 3

To make tassels (optional), thread needle with a double thread. Go through tip of star with thread (Diagram 1), and wrap 12 times around an inch-wide ruler (Diagram 2). Wrap needle end of thread around tassel approximately ¼" down from top (Diagram 3). Tie off with a couple of half knots. Thread a bell onto thread and, at each tassel, sew through tassel a couple of times to secure. Pull needle down through tassel, making 2 additional strings. Clip open other loops at bottom of tassel.

Woodland Log Tote

Instructions begin on page 125.

Pattern is full-size.

TREE PATTERN
Cut 3.

Ribbon Wreath

**Instructions begin
on page 24.**

8"-Wide Bow

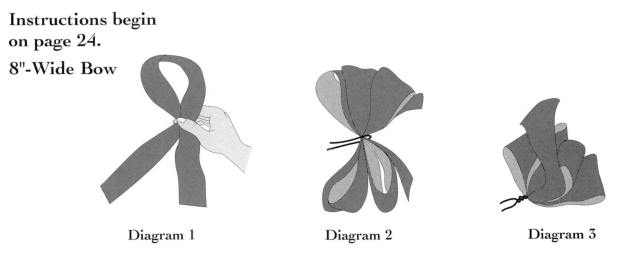

Diagram 1	**Diagram 2**	**Diagram 3**

For an 8"-wide bow, you will need 4 yards wire-edged ribbon. To make bow, measure 4" from end of ribbon. Pinch ribbon between forefinger and thumb (center point of bow). Make a 4" loop and pinch ribbon again at center (Diagram 1). Twist ribbon one-half turn and make a loop on opposite side. Make 5 loops on either side of the center in the same manner (Diagram 2). Fold 9" length of florist's wire over center of bow. Fold bow in half across wire. Holding bow firmly, twist wire ends together (Diagram 3). Fluff bow by pulling firmly on loops.

Ribbon Rose

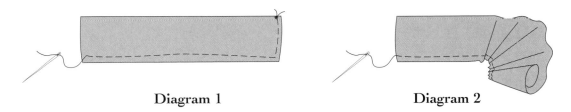

Diagram 1	**Diagram 2**

For each ribbon rose, working ¼" from edge, run gathering stitches down right edge and along bottom edge of ribbon (Diagram 1). Pull thread to gather tightly (Diagram 2). Roll gathered ribbon into rosette, tacking along bottom edge to secure.

Sources

Source information current at time of publication

Pages 8–17—Permanent florals, botanicals, and trees: Natural Decorations, Inc. (NDI), call (800) 522-2627 to find a retail store nearest you carrying NDI products.
Web site: www.ndihq.com
E-mail: ndi@ndihq.com

Page 14—Styrofoam cone: Schrock's, 110 Water St., P.O. Box 538, Bolivar, OH 44612, or call (330) 874-3700.

Pages 18 and 19—velvet cording: For information on stores carrying Grayblock ribbon, call (800) 847-8877.

beads: Beadbox Inc., 10135 East Via Linda #C116, Scottsdale, AZ 85258, or call (800) BEADBOX (232-3269).

Pages 20 and 21—tulle: For information on stores carrying Falk Industries tulle, call (212) 966-2800.

Styrofoam balls: Schrock's, 110 Water St., P.O. Box 538, Bolivar, OH 44612, or call (330) 874-3700.

Page 22—rubber stamps: Hot Potatoes Fabric & Wall Stamps, 209 10th Ave. So., #311, Nashville, TN 37204, or call (615) 255-4055.

Page 24—Styrofoam wreath: Schrock's, 110 Water St., P.O. Box 538, Bolivar, OH 44612, or call (330) 874-3700.

ribbon: For information on stores carrying Offray ribbon, call (908) 879-4700.

Page 40

Page 25—stickers: For information on stores carrying The Gifted Line stickers, call (800) 5-GIFTED.

Pages 26 and 27—chamois chandelier shades: Ballard Designs, 1670 DeFoor Ave. NW, Atlanta, GA 30318-7528, or call (800) 367-2810 for customer service.

Page 31—lady apples: Harry's Farmers Market, 1180 Upper Hembree Rd., Alpharetta, GA, or call (770) 664-6300.

Page 38—ribbon: Hyman Hendler & Sons LLC, 67 West 38th St., New York, NY 10018, or call (212) 840-8393.

tablecloth and napkins: Williams-Sonoma, 100 North Point Street, San Francisco, CA 94123, or call (800) 541-1262.

Page 40—paint: Suncoast Discount Arts and Crafts, 10601 47th Street North, Clearwater, FL 34622. Send $1 for a catalog or call (800) 340-4922.

Page 41—enamel glass paint: Look for Liquitex® Glossies™ Acrylic Enamel paint at art and craft stores.

Pages 42 and 43—beads: Beadbox Inc., 10135 East Via Linda #C116, Scottsdale, AZ 85258, or call (800) BEADBOX (232-3269).

Page 52—lady apples: Harry's Farmers Market, 1180 Upper Hembree Rd., Alpharetta, GA, or call (770) 664-6300.

Page 54—Styrofoam ring: Schrock's, 110 Water St., P.O. Box 538, Bolivar, OH 44612, or call (330) 874-3700.

Page 59—champagne mustard: look for Old Spice Champagne Mustard at local grocery stores, or contact Beaverton Foods, Inc., 4220 SW Cedar Hills Blvd., Beaverton, OR 97005.

tomato chutney: look for Alecia's Tomato Chutney at local grocery stores; or contact Alecia's Specialty Foods, 2332 Montevallo Rd., SW Leeds, AL 35094, or call (205) 699-6777.

Pages 62 and 63—deckle-edge scissors: Look for FISKARS® Paper Edgers at craft and fabric stores.

envelopes: For information on stores carrying The Gifted Line stationery, call (800) 5-GIFTED.

decorative metal corners and frame: Look for Creative Beginnings Brass Charms at local retail stores, or contact Creative Beginnings, P.O. Box 1330, Morro Bay, CA 93443, or call (800) 367-1739.

wallpaper: For information on stores carrying Waverly wallpaper, call (800) 423-5881.

Pages 64 and 65—felt: Look for Kunin Felt Classic Rainbow™ felt products at retail craft and fabric stores, or call (603) 929-6100 for mail-order prices.

Page 66—felt: Look for Kunin Felt Classic Rainbow™ felt products at retail craft and fabric stores, or call (603) 929-6100 for mail-order prices.

buttons: Look for JHB International buttons at retail craft and fabric stores, or call (303) 751-8100 to find the location nearest you.

Page 67—craft clay: For information on stores carrying American Art Clay products, call (800) 374-1600.

ribbon: For information on stores carrying Midori ribbon, call (206) 282-3595.

Page 68—charms: Look for Creative Beginnings Brass Charms at craft and fabric stores, or contact Creative Beginnings, P.O. Box 1330, Morro Bay, CA 93443, or call (800) 367-1739.

Page 69—stickers: For information on stores carrying The Gifted Line stickers, call (800) 5-GIFTED.

ribbon: Hyman Hendler & Sons LLC, 67 West 38th St.,

New York, NY 10018, or call (212) 840-8393.

Page 72—burlap packaging (Acaba open-weave burlap with gold threads): Contact Christmas & Co., Birmingham, AL at (205) 322-4646.

Pages 104–113—Fredericksburg Herb Farm, P.O. Drawer 927, Fredericksburg, TX 78624, or call (210) 997-8615.

Pages 106–113—Look for *Along the Garden Path* by Bill and Sylvia Varney at local bookstores, or call Fredericksburg Herb Farm at (210) 997-8615. Or, call Cookbook Marketplace at (615) 391-2661 for free catalog.

Page 106—essential oil and dried herbs: Tom Thumb Workshops, P.O. Box 357, 14100 Lankford Hwy., Mappsville, VA 23407. Send $1 for catalog or call (757) 824-3507.

Page 117—dried herbs: Tom Thumb Workshops, P.O. Box 357, 14100 Lankford Hwy., Mappsville, VA 23407. Send $1 for catalog or call (757) 824-3507.

fabric: For information on stores carrying Waverly fabric, call (800) 423-5881.

Page 121—velvet: For information on stores carrying Waverly fabric, call (800) 423-5881.

essential oil: Tom Thumb Workshops, P.O. Box 357, 14100 Lankford Hwy., Mappsville, VA 23407. Send $1 for catalog or call (757) 824-3507.

Page 122—Rub 'n Buff®: For information on stores carrying American Art Clay products, call (800) 374-1600.

Page 123—fabric: For information on stores carrying Waverly fabric, call (800) 423-5881.

wax crystals and precoated wicks: To order Candle Magic® products, call Brian's Crafts at (904) 672-2726. For information on stores carrying Candle Magic, call Distlefink Designs, Inc. at (201) 300-0400.

essential oil: Tom Thumb Workshops, P.O. Box 357, 14100 Lankford Hwy., Mappsville, VA 23407. Send $1 for catalog or call (757) 824-3507.

Pages 126 and 127—stamps, stamp pad, and embossing powder: Hot Potatoes Fabric & Wall Stamps, 209 10th Ave. So., #311, Nashville, TN 37204, or call (615) 255-4055.

Pages 128 and 129—lanterns: Contact Pottery Barn, at (800) 922-5507.

photo boxes: Contact Pier 1 Imports, Hoover, AL at (205) 733-8016.

Page 129—fruit ornaments: Contact Christmas & Co., Birmingham, AL at (205) 322-4646.

Page 136—cheesecloth: Look for cheesecloth at grocery and fabric stores; or contact Guardsman Products, Inc., Consumer Products Division, Grand Rapids, MI 49506.

Page 62

General Index

Page 43

Page 22

Recipe Index

Contributors

Designers

Kay Clarke, food gift wraps, 128–129

Janice Cox, shaving cream, hand scrub, aftershave, 116–117; tile boxes, 118

Virginia Cravens, food gift wraps, 128–129

Joe Gordy, AIFD, garland, 11; topiary, 14

Susan Harrison, original art, 31, 114–115

Linda Hendrickson, felt stockings and ornaments, 66

Margot Hotchkiss, ribbon wreath, 24; herbal bathtub tea, 122

Duffy Morrison, satin stockings, 18–19; tote bag, 116–117; stress-relief collar, 121; scented coasters, 123; log tote, 124

Joetta Moulden, text writer, 106–113

Lelia Gray Neil, star stamp, 26; painted cake dome, 40; painted plates, 41; painted pots, 115

Cecile Y. Nierodzinski, tulle garland, 20

Mary Benagh O'Neil, Hot Potatoes Fabric & Wall Stamps; imprinting velvet technique, 22; stamped Christmas card, 126; stationery gift set, 127

Dondra G. Parham, tablecloth, napkins, napkin rings, 38–39; memories album, 62; trinket box ornaments, 69; wreath pin and pendant, 120

Catherine B. Pewitt, ornaments, 21; fruit package toppers, 131

Adrienne E. Short, guest soap, 25; teacup candle, 123

Bill and Sylvia Varney, herbal recipes, 106–113

Patricia Weaver, picture frame, 68

Cynthia Moody Wheeler, velvet throw, 22; tree skirt, 65

Madeline O'Brien White, wire-wrapped tabletoppers, 43

Claudia Williams, craft clay ornaments, 67

Photographers

Jean M. Allsopp, 114

Ralph Anderson, 2–3, 24, 28–35, 68, 84, 118, 121–122, 130–131, left; 144

Jim Bathie, front cover, front flap, 4–5, 44–59, 71–73, 77–78, 80–83, 85–113, 128–129, 132–143

Randy Mayor, 70, 74–76, top

John O'Hagan, 8–23, 25–27, 36–43, 60–67, 69, bottom; 115–116, 120, 123–127, 131, right; 146, 151, 154, 156–157, back cover

Howard L. Puckett, 76, bottom

Deborah Safaie, 69, top

Photo Stylists

Kay Clarke, front cover, front flap, 4–5, 28–35, 44–59, 70–103, 128–129, 132–143

Joetta Moulden, 104–113

Katie Stoddard, 2–3, 8–25, 36, 38–43, right; 60–61, 64–69, 116–127, 130–131, 144, 146, 151, 156–157, back cover, top right and bottom

Linda Baltzell Wright, 26–27, 37, 43, left; 63, 115, back cover, top left

Acknowledgments

Thanks to the following people:
Blake Brinson
Lee Kinnebrew
E. D. Kirkland
Kathryn Nelson

Thanks to the following homeowners:
Pam and Tom Buck
Susie and Lew Burdette
Carolyn and John Hartman
Shannon and David Jernigan
Cecilia and Alan Matthews
Karen and Marshall Ross
Linda and Kneeland Wright

Thanks to the following businesses and organizations:
Creative Beginnings
Moro Bay, California
Ethan Allen
Vestavia Hills, Alabama
Greenbrier Furniture
Vestavia Hills, Alabama
The King's Ranch 1996 Showcase Home in Association with *Southern Living*®
Birmingham, Alabama
E. D. Kirkland, Kirkland Construction Company, Inc., Showcase Home in Association with *Southern Living*®
Montgomery, Alabama
Kohler
Nashville, Tennessee
Martin & Son Wholesale Florists
Birmingham, Alabama
Pearl Whirlpool Tubs, McCain Sales
Birmingham, Alabama
Waverly
New York, New York

CHRISTMAS CARD LIST

Name & Address	Sent	Name & Address	Sent